PRAISE FOR *THE BEST FLY FISHING IS EVERYWHERE*

"Robbins stands out for his ability to convey detail and abstractly riff and reflect on the broader fly fishing experience. This earnest, well-crafted collection of stories brings light to the fact that the people we fish with and the moments we share are often more memorable and important than the fish we catch."

—KEN MORRISH, co-founder of Fly Water Travel,
fly fishing photographer and writer

"Jesse Lance Robbins writes with the patience and precision of a seasoned angler. His sentences are clean, without wasted motion, and his stories linger in that liminal space between solitude and connection—where rolling a cigarette or changing a fly opens into something much larger. In *The Best Fly Fishing is Everywhere,* he finds grace in impermanence and meaning in what others might overlook. Don't expect answers. Expect company."

—STEVE DUDA, author of *River Songs: Moments of Wild Wonder in Fly Fishing*, head of Fish Tales at Patagonia, and former editor of *The Flyfish Journal*

"Jesse Lance Robbins has an eye for the unusual, the intriguing, and the downright surprising. Whether cataloguing obscene quantities of flies, delineating the precise qualities of a good cast, or simply sharing an old fashioned fishing tale, Robbins' eye for the unsung details that make fly fishing such a distinctive and special obsession is unmatched. The best fly fishing is indeed everywhere, because, as Robbins so artfully shows, the great thing about fly fishing is that it stays with us long after the flies have dried and we've stowed our rods."

—JASON ROLFE, editor of *The Flyfish Journal*

"It's obvious that fly fishing lives in Jesse's head just as much as it lives in his heart. Fly fishing stories from chasing big browns in New Zealand to tarpon in Florida and anadromous fish near the coasts, make it clear that yes, the best fly fishing is everywhere and Jesse joyously takes you along for the journey. Reading through each essay, you'll see his head and heart awake, alive, and anticipating his next encounter on a solo adventure or shared with loved ones. Sit down, grab a coffee, and enjoy this escape before planning your next adventure...everywhere."

—Kara Armano, editor of *TROUT Weekly*

"From Scotland to New Zealand, Bainbridge Island to Key West—Jesse Robbins' debut transports its reader as surely as a mountain stream carries an elk-hair caddis. Thanks to sharp detail and surprising turns of phrase, we're right on his shoulder as he casts for musky, Atlantic salmon, permit, Japanese seabass, cutthroat trout, Dean River steelhead, and so many others of this planet's most intriguing fish. In the end, you might just be persuaded: the world's best fly fishing exists everywhere that good friends, high adventure, and unflappable optimism converge."

—John Larison, bestselling author of *Whiskey When We're Dry* and *The Ancients*

"Jesse Robbins' essay collection, *The Best Fly Fishing is Everywhere*, focuses on the "why" of fly fishing instead of the where, when, and how—a crucial distinction in our Internet/social media era. It's a tenet I believe in so strongly that I founded a magazine based on it. Not that you won't learn things by reading Robbins' writing; from the unique pageant of a hex hatch in Maine to the thousandth cast for a musky or steelhead to the "dumb luck" of catching a permit, Robbins pleasantly describes the mix of joy and anguish found in the mental game of this beloved sport. He uses strong, surprising writing to inform, entertain, and enlighten his readers."

—Tom Bie, founder and editor of *The Drake Magazine*

THE BEST FLY FISHING IS EVERYWHERE

STORIES IN CELEBRATION OF WHY WE FISH

JESSE LANCE ROBBINS

Hatherleigh Press, Ltd.
62545 State Highway 10, Hobart, NY 13788, USA
hatherleighpress.com

THE BEST FLY FISHING IS EVERYWHERE

Library of Congress Cataloging-in-Publication Data is available.
ISBN: 978-1-961293-52-6

Interior design by Carolyn Kasper
Cover photography by Chase White
Interior art by Bre Drake

The authorized representative in the EU for product safety and compliance is Catarina Astrom, Blästorpsvägen 14, 276 35 Borrby, Sweden.
info@hatherleighpress.com

Versions of the following stories were previously published in print/online magazines: “Little Legs,” “At Night in the Surf,” “Floating with Barry,” “Perfectly Pacific Northwest,” “A Proper Taker,” “Biiru Kudasai,” “Swimmers,” “One Beer,” “Effortless & Pretty,” “Too Many,” “On Stealth,” “Contacts,” “The Day Begins the Night Before.”

Printed in the United States
10 9 8 7 6 5 4 3 2 1

For my parents.

CONTENTS

PART III: EVERYWHERE

INTRODUCTION: LITTLE LEGS

It's summer break and I'm nine years old—a shy, only child living on a dirt road in a small town. For the time being, my world consists primarily of my parents, a few best friends, and the family dog, and stretches as far as I can ride on my bike.

But there's a trout stream in the woods behind the house and I've bushwhacked there enough times to know the way to a few deep holes.

I got my first fly rod and reel for Christmas, a gift from my parents, so I spend a lot of my summer days on the river, fishing alone. As long as the dog and I are home for dinner, Mom and Dad are happy. There are a dozen flies in my one fly box, and I can't name any of them except the three that I recently tied, following instructions from the booklet in the beginner's fly tying kit that our neighbor gave me: a Mickey Finn, a black Woolly Bugger, and a Hare's Ear.

The dog and I have been crashing around for a while, getting distracted now and then by berry patches, salamanders, and what I think is poison ivy when we come to an inviting, shaded bend in the river. Studying my flies, which have been placed carefully in rows, I decide to tie on what I now know as a soft hackle, for no reason other than I haven't tried it before. My Dad's fishing buddy, affectionately known as "Uncle" John, gifted it to me. I don't yet know about water flows and temperatures and how they affect a trout's willingness to take a fly, so even though the water is low and warm, I just fish. I make the boring roll casts that Dad showed me, but soon enough, I'm trying to false cast and shoot line like he does. One out of five attempts goes pretty well and resembles a loop. There are 'wind knots' up and down my leader, but I don't notice or don't care.

I haven't seen any fish, as is usual when, from the depths of a dark pool, a trout that's eight inches long but might as well be thirty chases my fly at the end of a retrieve. As soon as it appears, it is gone. I repeat a curse that I heard someone at school say, then look over my shoulder to see if anyone heard me. I'm as excited as I've been since the last day of school, and I can't wait to tell my parents that I saw one. Maybe I'll tell them that I caught it.

I spend the next fifteen minutes casting to the same spot, expecting, hoping, wishing with all my might that the fish will come back and take my fly.

It doesn't, but it might tomorrow.

I'm back the next morning, just as soon as my little legs get me there.

PART I
HERE

FLY FISHING NEAR HOME,
WHEREVER THAT WAS
AT THE TIME

1

AT NIGHT IN THE SURF

Walking the beach in front of me is a silhouette barely darker than the horizon, and I follow while maintaining a close-but-consistent distance away. Though we both wear headlamps, neither is in use. In the absence of a clear visual, my hearing distinguishes his boots softly squishing over sand, then crunching and grinding on small stones, and then sliding and squeaking on top of large, seaweed-covered ledges. Then, a new sound: boots entering water. I stop, look up, and realize that we've reached our destination…at least, for now.

As a boy, I was raised a daytime angler. I was taught by my father that when it comes to fishing, one goes to bed early so they can then get up early and catch the morning bite. Staying up for a bite was also in play, but concluded promptly at dark for the previously mentioned reason. As I grew older and my fishing gained independence, 'early' and 'late' stretched into 'earlier' and 'later,' but I still conducted the business part of my angling during daylight. Then I befriended an angler whose approach fell far from my own; an approach based more on feel than feedback, more intuition than imitation, more consciousness than coincidence. An angling approach with higher stakes than simple recreation: night fishing.

"Remember the map I drew?" Pete asks. "This is the shallow boulder garden in the northeast corner."

Earlier in the day, he sketched a ten or so acre section of shoreline with no fewer than twenty landmarks and areas to fish. I tried to recall the specifics of this particular waypoint, looking into the dark for clues, but was given none in return. The task was much more straightforward on paper.

"Let me see your fly," he says, and I show him. "That's fine. The tide just turned, so the current is going to pick up soon. Swing your fly through all these currents and seams. As the water drops, wade further out so you can fish more of the boulder garden."

"Got it," I say, my confidence imperceptible.

"I'll be over there." Pete points into the night. "Yell if you need me."

He walks away, the sounds of his steps eventually overtaken by the soft crashes of waves and the ocean flowing over the rocks I'm about to fish. I take a hesitant step into the water, and another, my feet sliding over the bottom to make sure it doesn't fall out from underneath me. A few more steps and my right foot bumps into a boulder. I trace its outline with my boot and keep moving. Now knee-deep, I unhook my fly from a rod guide and flip it into the water. It disappears.

We decided that I would fly fish, even though Pete was sure that it was a less-productive method for this area. Our reasoning was that I'd be better off fishing a spot I didn't know with a technique I *did* know, as opposed to not knowing either. In any case, there's no debating that my own angling is compromised. Nevertheless, I begin.

At first, it feels like everything is inverted, like the world has turned upside down, and I'm fishing in a reflected ocean—as if I'm a mirror-image of myself, casting and fishing with my off-hand. Thankfully, the rod in my hand is not a new tool. I start short and am soon sending sixty feet comfortably into the unseen and unknown. What the fly does when it gets there is much less clear to me.

To a large degree, all fishing during the day is sight fishing in that you can see your fly, your lure, or your bait. You can see what it looks like in the water, you can see where it lands, and sometimes you can even see when a fish follows it. At night, however, sight is replaced by feel, and the learning curve that charts challenges and rewards is much steeper and reaches greater magnitudes. Without the benefit of sight, I'm required to visualize my fly in the water—not just what it looks like but how it's moving and where. It's difficult at first because it's new, but soon I'm no longer thinking about doing it; I'm just doing it. With no visual cues to tell me when a fish is near, I'm forced to fish each cast as if it is being followed. In my mind, I see and believe in each and every presentation.

As for Pete, he's doing what he knows best—surfcasting at this specific spot.

After a while, I hear him call my name. I turn and yell into the direction he'd pointed, and he responds from somewhere else.

"Doin' good?"

My response is swallowed by the night, but I acknowledge that I am in fact doing just fine.

Whereas fishing during the day sometimes makes time feel fleeting, at night, time doesn't just slow—it gets itself lost. Instead of running a losing race against the setting sun, we are drafting off the moon's soft glow, riding the night's camouflage and its intoxicating, comforting, and liberating effect on the fish. I know they're happy out there, and I'm sure that if my fly swings in front of one, it'll annihilate it.

A sudden inconsistency in the white noise of the wash raises an eyebrow and the hairs on the back of my neck.

"Let's move," I hear from behind me. I reel in and, while doing so, consider that I have no idea how long he's been standing there.

By now, my steps are surer and my eyes have fully adjusted to the color spectrum that spreads before us. Deep blues, purples, grays, and pitch black are the palette of this evening's painter, and our silhouettes slide in and amongst them as we make our way to another spot. I imagine us traversing Pete's hand-drawn map, and I'm now able to match his depictions to the terrain.

We arrive at our next location and drop our gear on a rocky beach. I know things have changed since we started fishing—the tide, moonlight, etc.— but why we're here, now, I understand only in concept. Pete has calculated these variables' intersection with the dead of night, and he begins fishing while I try to take in the new surroundings.

Intentionally, I haven't checked the time. I thought it would be amusing to lose track of it, but now that I'm out here and have also lost track of place, I'm not sure how it would help me, really. I do know that I'm tired. No surprise, as I haven't been awake at this hour since I don't know when. Fishing at night is habitual in the sense that it doesn't come easy at first and it requires the breaking of a competing habit to even engage in—sleeping, namely. But, like going to the gym or learning an instrument, at some point along the way, the activity loses its novelty, and it becomes more than a routine: it becomes a practice. Going night fishing just once is harsh on the body and the mind; that's where I'm at now. But the more frequently it's repeated, the easier it gets and the harder it is to stop, until it's just what you do; that's where Pete is.

I decide to take a break and see what I can learn by watching. Reclining against a smooth rock, legs crossed and hands behind my head, I study my friend fishing. Each cast is precise: a foot this way or that, his retrieves alternating between reeling, back-reeling, and letting his lure rise and swing in the current. It is clear that Pete is doing something much different than what I was doing with my fly, controlling his presentation in a way that I wasn't (and likely can't). I recognize that this is a function both of his equipment and his understanding of this place. It's said that the brighter the light, the more darkness you can see. In my case, the inverse has become true: the dark has illuminated what I do not know.

Suddenly, I perceive a change in his posture, and he sets the hook with his entire body. The rod arches into the night sky, line pointing into the abyss. Somewhere out there, a striped bass has been hooked. Pete takes off down the beach in pursuit, and I'm following him once again, keeping my distance as before, now so as not to interfere. I watch the fight with no idea where the fish is until he kneels to land it.

"Wanna see what they look like?"

The blues, purples, grays, and black of the night swirl yet again, as if slowly stirred together in a paint bucket. And in the middle of it all is me, my friend, and his fish.

2
HEXED

Even though I already had one that would've worked, the tent I found in a discount outdoor gear store was perfect for the trip Wilkie and I were planning: just big enough for two, ultra-packable, and incredibly lightweight. It was used, of course, but new enough that the original, informational hangtag was still attached. The price was so low that it seemed too good to be true, which, as it turned out, it was. I gave it a once-over before buying and set it up at home before we took off. It looked good enough to me.

Wilkie and I were trying to run into a hatch of Hexagenia limbata—'hexes,' for short. Hexes are giant, golden mayflies that emerge at dusk for several days or a week in late June and early July on certain ponds in northern Maine (and elsewhere around the country). The annual hatch is short-lived but truly a spectacle, comparable to the famous hatches of salmonflies and green drakes found out west. When a thick hatch comes off, trout rise repeatedly and recklessly, gulping these morsels from the water's surface before their wings dry and they fly off. The event also causes wiser and larger trout to be more daring than usual and feed off the surface more than they normally would otherwise.

It's impossible to predict the timing of such a hatch, but it's definitely worth trying for. Somehow, Wilkie caught wind of a certain pond—too remote and too small for most anyone else to know about or bother with—and pieced together intel on when the hexes there would hatch. It was a short hike to get in, but there was a small clearing with a primitive campsite on the shore. Topping it off, the pond was full of large, native brook trout.

It all sounds like that used tent, I suppose. But I've followed Wilkie and his angling intuitions on old logging roads, through brush, up and down riverbanks, and across brooks and ponds many times. We both grew up as only children in rural Maine and had an unspoken bond that quickly developed into a friendship founded in fishing and the journeys to and from the water. He's like an older brother to me, and I trust him on matters relating to fish, fishing, the outdoors, and life in general.

He's also a true jack-of-all-trades. He's a guy that can custom-build a house addition during the day, harvest a deer behind the house in the evening, process it that night, and cook an elaborate breakfast the next morning with the venison plus vegetables from his garden and eggs from his chicken coop. Then, before he leaves to coach his son's baseball game, he'll replace his truck brakes. All this is to say, I've looked up to him since we met and have learned a great deal from him over the years.

We arrived at the trailhead—essentially a game trail following the tiny outlet of the pond—at dusk, but the summer solstice had only just passed, so we still had plenty of light. Our packs were ready to go in the truck bed, filled with food, camping gear, waders, boots, deflated float tubes, and flippers.

Setting out, the heavy packs, uphill hike, and rapid pace quickly caught up to us, and we were soaked with sweat by the time we got our first view of the pond. Continuing our hurry-up-and-relax tempo, we tossed our packs on the ground and got to work setting up the tent, gathering firewood, pumping the float tubes, and prepping dinner. Soon, the only thing left to do was sit around the campfire, chat, and anticipate morning. Is the fishing ever as good as it was the night before? We settled into our sleeping bags, warm from whiskey and the fire. It was the best shape we'd be in until we got home.

Our dreams of a glass-smooth pond dimpled with rising trout dissolved as soon as we woke. We'd been socked in overnight, the pond having disappeared into the mist. A light breeze twisted the clouds around, distorting our depth perception and giving us only brief glimpses of the far shore. We hadn't been expecting cooler weather at all, so we reluctantly put on our remaining layers, strapped the fins on our wading boots, and kicked off.

The float tube I had was a loaner, one I hadn't had the luxury of trying beforehand. Settling in, I realized that the seat was well below the water line, so half my ass and thighs were submerged. This wasn't too bad in itself, unless...then my waders started leaking. Added together, this meant that most of my bottom half would be wet for the rest of the day. I took a mental inventory of my spare clothing, and noted I had exactly two remaining dry articles of lowers—one pair of underwear and cotton sweatpants. This seemed like a perfect problem to figure out later.

The cool weather kept any daytime hatch out of the question, and the breeze made fishing from the float tubes a chore, but we each had steady action on various streamers for most of the day. Gorgeous, feisty brook trout up to a foot long were feeding, and they were healthy, looking like there was plenty to eat in that little pond. The action was enough to keep my mind off the facts that I was now water-logged, chilled, and coming down with a cold.

Throughout the day, we held out hope that the weather would turn by the time evening came, bringing with it the flat-calm pond and thick hatch we'd spoken of while sitting around the campfire the night before. But the wind and rain only got worse, and eventually it was too late. We found reprieve underneath the tarp that we'd strung up and commenced to staring at a now-frothing pond. Our hopes simply weren't to be. Acceptance is sobering.

But whiskey isn't. By the time we burned all of the firewood, several hours had passed. We'd dried out, had dinner, finished the bottle, and still the rain hadn't let up. Passing out seemed the only thing left to do.

Climbing into the tent, it immediately became clear why it had been returned and sold at such a steep discount. Due to a design flaw, the now-saturated rain fly was resting directly on the tent itself, and water had been dripping through both onto our sleeping bags all day. Everything was soaked; crawling into my sleeping bag was just like sitting in that float tube with my leaky waders all over again. I fidgeted, trying to get comfortable, but every time I moved, I squished some water around, and another part of me got wet. Judging from his cursing, it didn't appear Wilkie's sleeping bag had fared any better. Whatever parts of us and our clothing that had dried and warmed while sitting around the fire were now wet and cold again.

As I lay there, I recalled a sales clinic I'd attended while working at a camping and fishing store in high school. The sales rep was explaining the benefits of synthetic insulation in sleeping bags. "While not as packable or lightweight as down," they said, "a synthetic bag will retain its warmth even if it gets wet." This all sounded fine, but I'd never been forced to test it out personally. I can now confirm that a wet synthetic sleeping bag does indeed insulate, but it's mostly a moot point, because it's exceptionally uncomfortable in a very unique, strange, and unsettling way. It's like being stuffed in a lukewarm, clammy, sticky, staticky plastic shopping bag.

Now it was pitch black, water falling from the tent ceiling onto us in our sodden sleeping bags. We were in for a long night. Remarkably, I fell asleep.

A deafening downpour awoke me, rain beating down on our tent fly while water steadily dripped on us. I sat up, short of breath. My nostrils were clogged and I could barely breathe. I needed to blow my nose, but there was no way that I was going to get out of that sleeping bag, because then I'd have to get back into it. I wrestled off my t-shirt, damp from the armpits down, held it to my face, and blew. Wilkie muttered and rolled over.

Eventually, the sky started to lighten. Everything was drenched. I worked my way out of the sleeping bag, exited the tent, and shuffled across the campsite until I was underneath the tarp. I put on a damp flannel, my raincoat, and dug out my last remaining piece of dry clothing, the sweatpants. It was drizzling. I was hungover and wholly sick. At least we could leave soon. Organizing gear, it occurred to me that Wilkie was still in the tent. This was curious because he's usually the first one up, no matter what happened the night before. Finally, I heard him stir (though it could've been that my non-stop snot rockets woke him up). As an attempt at solidarity, I plastered on a grin to greet him with and grabbed the empty whiskey bottle, as if I had just finished the last sip.

Wilkie stumbled out of the tent. We caught eyes, and the smile fell from my face. My joke was clearly not funny, and something was clearly very wrong.

"Water," he said hoarsely. I found a water bottle and handed it to him. He chugged, staggered back, and then looked at me with wide, wild eyes. I wasn't sure what was about to happen, but he was.

He spun around and dashed for the bushes but didn't make it halfway before projectile vomiting across the campsite and falling to his knees. I winced, watching while he convulsed and his nausea slowly passed.

When someone you've always thought invincible is in serious pain, it's shocking and scary. I remember as a young boy being woken up by my father limping into the house at night, howling in pain. He'd been playing basketball in the men's league and took a severe charley horse. It was hard to understand how something could hurt someone so strong, so badly.

In Wilkie's case, a migraine had come on over the course of the night. He told me later that it felt like someone was driving 16 penny framing nails into his temples. Between the weather and the vomiting episode, we'd had it. Type Two Fun wasn't a foreign concept to us, but this was testing the limit. We broke camp in silence. I don't remember a single step of the hike out, but when we made it to the truck, Wilkie finally spoke again.

"You gotta drive," he said, tossing me the keys. "And stop at the first gas station you see."

Even this seemingly routine request was way out of character for Wilkie. He woke up as we pulled in. I grabbed a cup of coffee, a breakfast sandwich, and a stack of napkins and went back to the truck. A few minutes later, he came out with a full shopping bag, and emptied the contents onto the bench seat: orange juice, ginger ale, Gatorade, Tylenol Cold & Flu, Advil, Tums, and Ricolas. I blew my nose. We looked at each other and shook our heads at what we saw.

An hour further down the road, with the end of the trip finally and plainly in sight, we began to laugh. We'd rapidly descended from the precipice of angling fortune to the depths of backpacking defeat, but neither of us would begin to deny that it wasn't worth trying. And we couldn't say for certain that we wouldn't do it all over again. We added it to our ever-growing collection of adventures and misadventures, a testament to a brotherhood born on the water and in the woods.

Soon, we were scheming again. After all, the hexes would hatch any day.

3

ONE, TWO, THREE

The air is quiet. The day, half-asleep. Every noise—our whispers, birdsong, a knock on the boat, the click of fly reel—is felt and feels too loud. Current pulls us downstream so slowly that it feels like we're drifting on a river of molasses.

I dip the oars in the water just deep enough and just quick enough to hold us in place, adjusting our angle by two or three degrees with each stroke. We look into the shallows and watch as a small wake glides leisurely between patches of grass, through lily pads, under a downed tree, and among small boulders. We can't see the fish itself but know exactly where it is, and where it's going.

The sun isn't high enough to hit the water, but a few beams make it through the elm trees and land on our faces and chests. The early-morning respite from the heat and humidity is all but gone, and I can feel beads of sweat starting to form on my back. This is my favorite time of day, that brief, passing period between the cool of night and the hot of the day.

We hear muffled voices behind us. I look back and see the other boat, on anchor in the middle of the river, in perfect position to cast at the dead tree that's poking its old, waterlogged trunk out of the water by eight inches. Underneath, a big bass surely awaits in ambush.

I can imagine the conversation taking place between our two friends in the boat, each of them too polite to make the first cast of the day and too stubborn to submit to the argument that they should make it. The fact that there are twenty or more such trees (and bass) in the stretch of river ahead does not affect their current deliberation.

In my boat, we have passed the debate on who will fish first—I won by playing the "Hey, you're the guest" card—and we are now moments away from the first cast. We are waiting for this little smallmouth bass to swim into an area no bigger than a windshield, a specific spot where we can make a cast in between overhanging tree limbs. It's on its way, but taking its time, stopping to eat a neon blue damselfly here and there. We are content to watch and wait.

For a moment, we lose track of the bass as it swims behind a rock. It reappears in what cannot be more than four inches of water and is about to enter our windshield of opportunity. My fishing partner starts casting at the exact same time as I say, "Yup."

The little deer hair popper splats down on the water two feet in front of the bass. The instant it hits the water, the bass races over and takes it as if it's the first meal it has seen in a week and it's about to fly away. The bass is all of nine inches long but gives a noble pull before being brought to hand. We let it go and it races away again, out of sight.

Quietly, slowly, we open the cooler and remove two ice-cold beer cans. Glancing back to confirm that we are undetected, we see that the two in the other boat still haven't agreed upon who will make the first cast; they may never, though one will eventually make it. We ready our forefingers on the tabs, and softly count, 'One, two, *three.*' The synchronized opening sounds like a giant, amplified cricket, and the discharge reverberates across the flat river, through the still air and slaps the others in their faces.

The occupants of the other boat whirl around in their seats just as fast as that little bass racing to take the deer hair popper. Then they watch as we drink from the beer cans as if they're the first drinks we've seen in a week and they're about to fly away.

4
FISHING WITH HARRY

We'd never met, but I recognized him immediately. He was timeless, white hair and wrinkles contrasting a youthful glow, springy step, and rugged physique. Probably too old to be my father, he also appeared too young to be my grandfather. Between his knee-high rubber boots, faded navy coveralls, sun-scorched hat, and deep tan, he undoubtedly looked salty.

He seemed to recognize me, too, but it probably wasn't difficult: my old Toyota van, the stereotypical vehicle of the traveling foreigner, was the only one of its kind in the parking lot. I don't remember what I was wearing, exactly, but it's safe to assume my appearance was out of place as well—a wardrobe resulting from limited space, a specific purpose (which wasn't this one), and my own eclectic personal tastes, which were obviously different from everyone else's at the marina.

Harry's hand dwarfed mine in a firm handshake with rough calluses that made me feel adolescent and inferior. It was clear his hands had worked many, many more hours than mine. He didn't have much to say but was polite, asking if I found the place alright and instructing me on where to stash my gear. His boat was an eighteen-foot aluminum dual console, and he'd neatly placed four spinning rods in rod holders at the stern. They were rigged, save for bait, which I noted was on ice in a plastic bucket nearby. Stashed under the gunwale was a gaff, along with a few coiled ropes and life jackets. I appreciated the organization.

Then we did the whole guest/host boat launching dance, wherein the guest tries to be of help and exhibit that they know what they're doing, but mostly ends up getting in the way and making the process more complicated for the host. I was a few months into my New Zealand trip at this point, and I'd been put in touch with Harry by the couple that I was staying with—friends of family friends. It was a thoughtful arrangement and a nod to the much-lauded Kiwi way of hospitality. But I've found that being introduced by your passion or preoccupation—be it fishing, music, dance, art, whatever—yields mixed results.

On the one hand, when you identify primarily as a doer of whatever it is that you love, it signifies your prioritization of that thing in your life, which suggests that you may be wise enough to understand what fulfills you. It's also assumed that you have studied and practiced your craft enough to achieve some level of competency, perhaps even expertise. On the other hand, your aptitude for the avocation may suggest a reluctance toward obligation, which could land hard. And, unless the person you're being introduced to is *also* an angler, musician, dancer, etc., they may form an idea of you based on their conception of that activity—no fault of their own, but also not wholly accurate of you. For non-anglers (like the folks I was staying with), fishing is often just fishing. By that, I mean they aren't aware of—again, by no fault of their own—the drastically different types and styles of fishing, or the potentially differing philosophical views of fishing that exist among anglers.

In other words, just because Harry and I both claimed to be "fishermen" didn't ensure that we'd be on the same page when we got on the water together. That's a lovely thing about fishing: we can choose to do it how we want to. But that same freedom, unfortunately, comes with the potential consequence that some anglers will disagree with another's chosen methods. In most instances, we agree to disagree, and wish each other good fishing. But in the extreme cases, these disagreements can lead to confrontation. It sounds silly—and it is, to some degree—but these are deeply personal passions and we are very serious about them. This is most apparent when the emphasis on catching fish varies from one angler to another; a misalignment of intentions can be disastrous to the experience for all parties.

As it turned out, Harry's intentions weren't the only ones I had to worry about, for as I left the house that morning, I was surprised by Ian, my host, handing me an ice-filled cooler. I responded to the gesture with a look of confusion.

"That's for your fish, mate," he said, amused at my misunderstanding. "We're counting on you for dinner!"

Catching dinner wasn't unfamiliar to me—I'd fished for meat and filled coolers before. What was abnormal was the *expectation* of catching it. Sometimes, all that can be done while fishing is to simply fish well; going into things with the expectation of catching fish isn't always the best idea. But from Ian's perspective, it made perfect sense: a fisherman catches fish, so what better time to have a freshly-caught dinner?

This all weighed on me as I drove to meet Harry, but he wasn't the least bit phased when I arrived carrying the empty cooler.

Our target that day was blue cod; we'd be bottom-fishing for them with cut bait amongst the coral. The plan was to drift with the current, drop lines, and sooner or later, we'd feel a tug, hook the fish, and reel it in. It was certainly a different approach from what I had been doing on trout rivers, and while the method seemed somewhat unsophisticated, I knew well that dinner wasn't going to put itself in the ice box.

The minimum length was fourteen inches, and the limit was three apiece. Based on the tone with which he delivered this final piece of information, I gathered that Harry had hit this limit many times before and intended to do so again today. His confidence was infectious, and I envisioned returning to the marina with our coolers full of cod filets.

The sea was a magnificent aquamarine color, almost as blue as the sky. Even though the day was young, the sun was bright and warm. Islands of sheer cliffs topped with lush greenery rose from the water and floated on the horizon. I'd forgotten how much I loved being on the ocean with the wind in my face. I realized that it was the first time I had seen New Zealand from the sea, a very different perspective than any I'd had so far, unachievable from any hiking distance.

After a twenty-minute run, Harry slowed the boat, checked the depth on his electronics, and then killed the engine. I rubbed sunscreen onto my nose and face and offered him some. He waved it away, and I realized that it had probably been years since he last applied any. We began drifting as Harry started slicing small squid for bait. Then he grabbed one of the baitcasters, baited the hook, and handed the rod to me.

My father put a fishing rod in my hands for the first time when I was four years old. Five years later, I started learning to fly fish, and since then, I've spent much less time with other types of fishing rods. I'm competent with a fly rod, but I'm definitely uncomfortable with a spinning or casting rod in my hand. My understanding of these tools is limited, and I've never fished well with either one.

I looked up and down the rod as if the instructions were printed on it somewhere. Sensing my hesitation, Harry spoke. "Cast it out a way, let it sink to the bottom, then bring it up a few feet."

I reared back and prepared to cast.

"And keep your thumb on the line as it goes out so that it doesn't get in a big mess," he added.

The reminder was timely—I was about to do just that—and I made my cast, trying not to look like I hadn't touched a casting rod in years. The big sinker splashed down; I avoided a big mess. I even surprised myself at the distance.

"You don't need to cast so far," Harry said. "You might lose your bait, and the weight will bring it all back under the boat anyway. And try not to cast in the direction we're drifting."

This was some fisherman he'd been given for the day, he was no doubt thinking. If there had been any question as to my experience in this style of fishing before, it was clear now that I had no idea what I was doing. I watched Harry make his cast, let his bait get to the bottom, reel in a bit, and then sit, facing the stern. Placing his left foot on the starboard gunwale, he assumed a reclined-yet-ready position that I could tell he'd spent countless hours in. Like any master of their craft, he made it look easy and inspired imitation. I adjusted my posture accordingly.

I don't recall who spoke first, but eventually someone broke the ice and we shared brief recounts of our lives. The conversation inevitably turned to fishing, and I learned that in his younger days, Harry had spent a lot of time doing what I came to New Zealand specifically to do: hiking in the bush to fly fish for trout. At the time, it baffled me that anyone would trade sight-fishing for giant, spooky brown trout and bottom-fishing for blue cod, but I recognize now that I've no right nor basis to rank angling methodologies. Looking back on it, I see the appeal: it's simple in theory but nuanced in practice, quiet and contemplative, with a meal (or perhaps the gift of one) afterward. Plus that distinct feeling of captaining your own vessel.

The bite was slow at first, and Harry adjusted our location several times. At each spot, he checked our depth and position relative to several islands or landmarks on shore. I could tell that he was performing computations in his head, but I never knew what kind, exactly. Our conversation faded in and out, but the silences weren't awkward—by this point, we were both intent on the mission. I was starting to get the hang of the fishing (or at least the casting) when I missed a strike. Harry saw it happen and offered concise, constructive feedback on my technique.

Eventually, I hooked one and reeled in a modest specimen of our intended quarry. After measuring the fish and confirming it met regulations, Harry placed it carefully in the cooler. Then he stuck out his hand and smiled for the first time. We shook, this time as friends and equals, no longer strangers, and exchanged a look of two anglers who knew that the bite was now on.

The pressure to catch dinner was gone, and I started to gain a sense of confidence. And, as is often the case, with that confidence came a few more fish to the boat. They weren't all keepers; Harry was strict on his measurements. At one point, I reeled in one that was considerably larger than any we'd yet seen—seventeen or eighteen inches and plump. Harry was impressed and commended me on the fish. I felt a swelling of pride, taking his remark as a testament to my angling skills. It only took missing the next three strikes to remind myself that I still didn't know what I was doing.

We were at what would be our last spot of the day when Harry hooked a fish that immediately bent his rod like no other had. He was quick on his feet, following the fish around the boat as it circled beneath us. I moved around as he did, trying my best to stay out of the way.

As the fish tired, Harry gained line, and we got our first look at it. It appeared to be some type of shark, roughly three feet long. I stepped back as it thrashed boatside, offering a plain view of its wide mouth and rows of teeth.

"What now?!" I yelled.

"We kill it," Harry replied straight away. "The sharks eat the cod."

Without warning, he handed me the rod, bent over the gunwale, stuck his hand into the water, and came up with the twisting shark by the tail. He tossed it on the deck, then grabbed a small, baseball bat-like club with a large nail embedded through the middle of it. I hadn't noticed it before, but the few inches of spike that stuck out of the side meant only one thing.

"Look out!" he yelled.

I watched as he brought down the spiked club on the shark. A neat hole appeared on the top of its head. Again, the club went down. And again. Finally, the shark stopped thrashing. Harry grabbed it by the tail again and, like a frisbee, threw it over the side of the boat. The shark spun in the air until it splashed down, and the blue-green water started turning to deep red. The stain dispersed around the floating shark, now belly-up, like cranberry juice wicking across a paper towel. We both watched in silence as it slowly drifted away.

I never would have guessed that the quiet man I'd been spending the day with had...*that* in him. Harvesting cod for dinner was one thing, but killing the shark seemed extreme and totally unnecessary. I shot a glance at Harry. He was still staring at the dead, floating shark, now fifty yards away.

"I guess I didn't have to kill it," he said finally, a touch of regret in his tone.

If I offered some sort of consolation, I don't remember what it was.

The shark eventually floated out of sight and out of mind. Our focus returned to the fishing. The bite was still on, and soon we were in good spirits again. Before I knew it, six legal cod lay on ice in the cooler. Slowly, we broke down the gear and made ready for the run back to shore. Taking one last look around the boat and at our surroundings, we nodded to each other, acknowledging a job well done and a day well spent. Harry fired the motor, put it in gear, and pointed us toward the marina.

As we ran, my thoughts drifted back to the dead shark. It was a piercing image, seeing it float away in its crimson cloud—one that I didn't enjoy. But it was also a necessary and sobering reminder of the consequences of putting hooks into the mouths of fish. While I had released every trout that I caught in New Zealand, it's likely that at least one died after swimming away, possibly more. Just like that shark, those trout perished for no real good reason other than my own selfish motives.

I expected to part ways with Harry after reaching the marina, but he instead insisted that I join him and his wife for lunch at their home. Apparently, lunch was part of the plan all along—another curiosity considering that we were intending to fish until we caught our limit. Yet by the time we arrived, Harry's wife Betty had already set their patio table. I'm still perplexed on how the timing of it all fell into place—go catch dinner but be back for lunchtime—but maybe I was just too far removed from fishing expectations and schedules by that point in my travels.

Betty was the nicest Kiwi anyone could meet, and she took to me like a grandmother would. Over sandwiches and iced tea, she, Harry, and I chatted the afternoon away in the sun. Before I left, Harry filleted the cod and repacked the cooler with fresh ice, while Betty sent me off with freshly baked cookies. They'd thought of everything.

During my time in New Zealand, I was skunked as much as I was successful. Even successful days often involved landing just a single trout. I quickly learned to cherish every fish that I encountered, but trout fishing with the intent of releasing whatever I caught meant that the stakes were low, the consequences essentially nil, if I didn't land one on any given day. Sure, I had nerves when approaching and casting to the large brown trout that I spotted, but no one was waiting for me at the end of the day, expecting a filet to fry. Angling alone, I didn't have anyone to answer to whenever I went fishless, nor celebrate with whenever I did land one.

Fishing with Harry was different. By the time we met, I'd become so accustomed to getting skunked by myself that the exercise of having to catch dinner to share with others was completely foreign, if not illogical. Yet with those cod filets in the cooler, I felt a distinct sense of accomplishment and relief that I hadn't had while trout fishing.

When Harry and I said our goodbyes, it felt like we'd known each other for years, though it had barely been a day. Maybe it was a function of our circumstances: me, a young and eager traveler who'd been fishing solo, and him, an experienced and settled angler whose children had left home. Regardless, the real bond was formed by our time on the water together, however brief, in pursuit of our common goal.

For Harry, it was probably just another day. The task wasn't especially demanding, dangerous, or critical, and didn't even require the two of us to be successful, but there was no denying that it was made better by sharing it. In the end, fishing is just fishing.

When I returned to Ian's that afternoon, I proudly presented the full cooler to my hosts, and we all enjoyed fresh fish and chips for dinner that night. Yet far more memorable than the meal was fishing with Harry and the lessons we shared. I never saw him again and likely won't, but I can still picture Harry fishing in his little boat, reclined-yet-ready, quietly and confidently catching his limit of blue cod for dinner with Betty.

5
SECRET TROUT POND

"*The door will be open. Make yourself at home. You'll see we have a small pond on the property too. I think there may be fish in it!*"

That was the last email I'd received from my future landlord before starting the drive from Colorado to Washington. I'm not sure if I gave the statement a second thought at the time; it just seemed too fantastical.

I was twenty-seven and, following a few years of transience and minimal income, had just accepted a full-time job in the fly fishing industry on an island in Puget Sound. I'd been guiding in southwest Colorado, and I secured the housing through a kind, soon-to-be coworker, who put me in touch with a couple who had a studio for rent. It was furnished, inexpensive, and available immediately—ideal for a seasonal fishing guide about to re-enter the real world. The landlords also didn't seem to have any problems with me paying the first month's rent in the small bills I'd collected in tips, which was convenient.

A week later, after turning what could've been a 1,300-mile drive into 2,500 to visit friends and fish, I arrived...and sure enough, there was the pond, barely visible in the evening light. The next morning, after sleeping off the drive, I walked to the bay window of my new abode, looked at the water, and to my delight, saw a rise.

Though, perhaps I shouldn't have doubted. From the start, the move to Bainbridge Island felt scripted. It's not a common place to travel to, let alone move to, yet oddly enough, I'd visited it before. Several years prior, fresh off my extended trip to New Zealand, I'd traveled up and down the West Coast by way of Craigslist's "rideshare," an organized hitchhiking message board. I went from Los Angeles all the way up to Seattle, crashing with friends along the way.

In addition to seeing familiar faces, I was also interested in scouting out a few towns and cities as potential places to move. In Seattle, with a day to myself, my hosts suggested that I take a Washington State Ferry across the Sound to Bainbridge. It was March, and I remember standing on the passenger deck, facing the wind. Though I'd never boated on the Pacific, the voyage felt oddly nostalgic. I was reminded of sailings aboard Casco Bay Lines ferries in Portland, Maine, and early-morning, offshore departures from Waquoit Bay in Cape Cod. I breathed the salty air deep, watched the ferry landing approach, and smiled. I found a path along the harbor, which eventually led to a restaurant, and I had lunch on the patio in the sun. If someone had told me then that I'd be a resident of the island in a few years, I think I would've just nodded. Anything seemed possible at the time.

Coming from Colorado, where I lived in a cabin less than a hundred feet from an amazing trout stream, the move to Bainbridge was a compromise in terms of my proximity to traditional fly fishing water. But the job was worth it, and I accepted that I'd be traveling more than before to fish in the way—and frequency—I'd become accustomed.

So, when the email came in about the pond, I simply didn't believe it. There has to be a catch when taking a job you've dreamed about. Surely the studio, property, and pond weren't also going to be the stuff of dreams.

The homestead sits in a depression in the approximate center of the island at the end of a dead-end dirt road. There is no traffic on this road. You have to know exactly where you're going to even find it; it essentially doesn't exist to anyone who doesn't already know that it's there. For these reasons, the pond came to be known as the *Secret Trout Pond,* or STP for short. The degree to which its existence is held private is debatable, but the moniker adds a layer of simple mystery any angler can appreciate. Over the years, it built up a reputation not dissimilar from *Fight Club*: the first rule of Secret Trout Pond is that you do not ask to fish Secret Trout Pond.

The house is built into a hill and the studio is on the ground floor. The entrance to the studio, its windows, and a patio all face the pond. Inside, a small dining table also served as a fly tying desk and laptop station, plus was a perfect vantage point of the pond. While eating, tying, or writing, whenever the rises became too frequent to ignore, I'd grab a rigged rod from its perch above the door and in twenty steps, be fishing.

Mallards frequented the pond, as did a great blue heron. On one memorable morning, while a friend and I sat on the patio eating breakfast, a healthy, eight-point blacktail buck walked out of the woods, down to the pond for a drink and a look around, then continued on his way. According to the landlords, STP has never been stocked. In my interpretation, this means that the pond's small cutthroat residents are of the coastal variety (*Oncorhynchus clarkii clarkii*), but they became landlocked at some point.

Simply having a body of water on the property where one lives is special enough, and one with some sort of catchable fish in it is about as good as it gets. But add to that a native trout population? And to *that*, a strain unique to only that pond? It's almost too much. There were even rumors of adult coho salmon reaching the pond on spawning runs of the past.

The fish in STP are, to steal a phrase from a friend, "agreeable to fly presentations." Most small dry flies work, which keeps things simple. Foam grasshopper patterns will raise fish, but the cutthroat have a hard time getting their jaws around the bigger bugs. Weighted nymphs and small streamers work as well, though after a day of sub-surface experimentation in an attempt to locate larger specimens, I started bringing dry flies only (we didn't find any big ones). Picky eaters or not, they are incredibly beautiful. Their crimson cuts meet with translucent, rosy-pink-purple cheeks; their backs are green-tinted silver. The largest one I landed, based on a guesstimate referencing a photo of the fish in my hand, was between eight and nine inches. Despite their size, they do not appear to be juvenile fish, just stunted by the small pond. In looking at pictures, were any size references removed, one might guess that they were sixteen inches long.

A mowed lawn separates the studio and the pond, providing ideal backcast space. There's a short dock extending into the pond from the lawn, and I could usually raise the fish hiding beneath if I approached quietly, made my first cast from far enough away, landed most of the fly line on the grass, and presented the fly within six inches of the dock. A large alder hangs over the water along the southern shore of the pond, and from the dock itself, an accurate, forty-foot sidearm cast puts a fly neatly under the old rope swing that hangs from the tree. Being in the Pacific Northwest, the rope is usually waterlogged and so drips onto the pond; the droplets' rings on the water tricked me and most other anglers who visited. There are some downed trees on the far shore, surrounded by cattails and tall grass, providing some intriguing cover to try to cast into as well. On windy days, leaves and duckweed flow across the pond and back, opening and closing windows to cast into. Sometimes on calm days, rises dimple the pond all day long.

Slowly and cautiously, I began to share STP with close friends and colleagues. In Washington, our favorite target quarry was steelhead, but fishing for them often left us skunked and mentally exhausted. STP became a welcome respite from long, encounter-less weekends on the Olympic Peninsula. Usually, a long lunch was plenty of time for a couple of people to heal their wounds from the coastal rivers and get enough of a fish-catching fix enough to consider trying to hook a steelhead again.

We came to know STP well. We learned which weather would cause the fish to rise the most or put them down. We discovered which flies worked best for given conditions and found out how the fish responded to the presented patterns. We knew the best places around the pond's perimeter to cast from and, at each, knew the casting angles that the surroundings allowed. If there wasn't a fish under the rope swing, there might be one along the tall grass just past it. A good backhanded or left-handed cast from the dock might catch a fish between the downed limbs on the right bank. The shallow cove in the southwest corner, which appeared to have an underground outlet, held fish, but the banks were steep there, making it challenging to land the fish properly without getting wet. On clear, sunny winter days, text message chains would begin before we got to work: "*STP lunch?*" We started calling in to-go lunch orders and picking them up on our way to STP.

We also came to understand and appreciate how unique and special STP was. None of us heard of any other place like it, on the island or beyond. We shared it with a few guests from out of town but never overstayed our welcome. We never fished it more than once every couple of weeks for fear of affecting the population or the fish getting wise to our flies; neither effect came to pass. The more we visited it, the longer our stays became, but the less we actually fished.

A wiser angler once told me that there's a difference between *going places* and *knowing places*. I think I knew this subconsciously, but it had never been put to me in such plain and simple terms. The crux lies in the frequency of visits, which is a direct function of proximity. Having a home water, one to return to often, allows for a magnitude of observations that cannot be gained by visiting once or twice, or even once a year. And beyond the sample size of visits, it's the variety of the visits themselves. To see a fishery over the seasons, over the years, and in its many forms and moods, is to truly know it.

Going places and knowing places; neither one is better than the other, but it takes experience in both to fully appreciate what each offers. We can still treasure and enjoy the places that require long travel times to get to, but to understand a place, it has to be nearby and seen often. To approach the water with our own ever-changing emotions and perspectives, to listen to it, learn from it, and give back to it, is to have a relationship with it, just like knowing a person.

Unfortunately, it's impossible to write, call, or text a river, a pond, or a flat and ask how they're doing. This is perhaps why 'fishing reports' are so popular. We ought to use a less surgical-sounding name, though. It's more like 'thinking of you.'

6
FLOATING WITH BARRY

Moonlight revealed glimpses of the river below as I wound along the canyon road. New to Washington, I was making my way for the first time to the Yakima River—a Columbia tributary in the south-central part of the state. It's always exciting to wake up somewhere that you've never been and even more so when that somewhere is next to a river you've never fished before. Perhaps *too* exciting because when I first made out the distance from the road down to the water, I realized that I was driving way too fast.

By the time I got to the campground, it was well after dark. Organizing some gear, I overheard my neighbors discussing the day's fishing. Their campfire was burning, so I wandered over. Scattered around the site were four beat-up tents, a half-dozen rickety camp chairs, a stack of river rafts of various sizes, a truck-bed trailer, a generator powering a flood light, and a slew of miscellaneous camping equipment. There I met Barry, the site's occupant, and another camper, Jim. I introduced myself and asked about the fishing.

Barry's report was lengthy. Born and raised in the town of Yakima, Barry claimed to have floated the river more than five hundred times. Two days before, he'd caught twenty-five, he told me, and did so by fishing a modified Rooster Tail spinner, cutting off two of the three hooks to satisfy regulations. He said that he didn't care much for fly fishing, since the goal of fishing was to catch as many fish as possible. Jim politely tried to defend the sport of fly fishing, but Barry wasn't having it. I stayed quiet, not wanting to take sides on what I could see would be a fruitless argument.

Barry didn't seem to have any trouble carrying on a conversation by himself though, sharing fishing information and opinions for anyone who would listen. I couldn't decide if he was drunk, stoned, or worse. I'd come across some similar folks before, and my policy is to approach carefully, if at all. But when they so readily offer fishing insights, I also find it's hard to walk away. Safe to say that everything that comes out of their mouths isn't true, but exactly which parts are false or how much the truth is stretched is tough to gauge.

In this case, I doubted that Barry had floated the Yakima five hundred times but, assuming that he did indeed grow up nearby, I suppose it's not inconceivable. In any case, he'd certainly spent some significant time on the river.

After chatting for a while, Barry offered to take me on a float the next day. It was a tempting proposal considering my inexperience there: a float down a new river with a veteran angler. I envisioned catching three fish on my flies to his one; or worse, his twenty on Rooster Tails to my zero. I politely declined, saying that I preferred to wade-fish my first day, but maybe we could float together the following.

The next night, Barry appeared at my campsite. He observed my stack of hand-sawed firewood and remarked, "You're pretty self-sufficient, kid. Just like me." Over the next couple of hours, we talked about the Yakima, Washington, fishing, and life. Apparently, Barry used to be regarded as a "top snagger" in his hometown. He told me how he once spotted a large steelhead from a bridge, snagged it (from the bridge), fought it to its death, then hand-lined it up to his perch. He spoke of the various wildlife found around the canyon and had me follow him to a specific part of the campground where, with a spotlight, he showed me a great horned owl in a big pine tree.

When I told him that I'd caught a dozen fish over the course of the day, his opinion on fly fishing seemed to change, and he wanted to see my fly boxes. "I can tell that you know how to fish, just looking at your flies," he said. "I haven't tied any in a while…"

For every couple of statements or opinions that would make me shake my head in disbelief or disgust, he'd offer one that I respected. So, despite his stories and my misgivings, I decided to join him for a float after all. I'd see some new water, in any case.

We combined supplies the next morning and tucked in for a big breakfast. While we ate, Barry showed me some fish pictures on his digital camera, and I began to have second thoughts about the day's float. Barry's "two-man raft" looked to be designed more for pool leisure than fly fishing on moving water. Now in the daylight, I also noticed the state of Barry's gear: all his tents had holes in them, while two had doors with broken zippers. He told me with more than a hint of pride how he had found it all in dumpsters or abandoned along the river. By this point, I was becoming much less enthused by the idea of spending four or five hours together in a small raft.

After further discussion and some attempts to get out of the whole thing, I agreed on a shorter float than initially planned—five miles, ending at the campground. At the put-in, Barry pumped up his raft while I tried to look unaffiliated. Finally, we were off, and I was relieved to discover that his vessel held air.

Shortly into our trip, he spied a beer can on the far shore and rowed over to it. I assumed he was collecting it for supplementary income, but it turned out that Barry was more interested in the contents. That can was empty, but he assured me that rafters often lose full beers, and ten minutes later we were on shore again. On our sixth beer can stop, Barry found a full one and promptly drank it. A belch of satisfaction echoed off the canyon walls.

Soon, Barry hooked his first rainbow, and I began to worry that I was about to be severely out-fished. But it turned out Barry wasn't about competition; he was about having a good time. Despite his constant profanity, he was in great spirits, and when I got my first fish, he was ecstatic, asking what it ate and where. "I knew we'd both catch fish, man!" he exclaimed.

Barry's casual outlook extended to a relaxed view on rowing. We spun three-sixties, drifted through prime runs, cut off drift boats, bounced off rock walls, and zigzagged our way downstream, all the while investigating beer cans and flotsam on the river's edge.

At one point, we approached good-looking water, and I was in the midst of a decent drift.

"Get ready," Barry said. "I always get one in here."

Sure enough, a few seconds later I was tight to my biggest fish of the weekend. Barry skillfully rowed us into slack water where I landed a gorgeous wild rainbow. I obliged his request for a photo and smiled as the fish swam off. Barry hollered. I suggested that he take up guiding.

The next time Barry began rowing toward shore, it wasn't for a stray beer can or to land a fish. "I gotta take a crap… you got any TP?"

I said I didn't, and a moment later Barry was twenty feet upstream, a couple yards from the water, squatting with his pants around his ankles. I looked away and prayed that the drift boat we'd just passed did not come around the bend. When he got back to the boat, he pushed us off into the current before holding out his hand and offering me a Tootsie Roll.

Barry's constant chatter continued throughout the day, ten of his words to every one of mine. I couldn't help but think that he was probably a little lonely and wondered when he had last fished with anyone else. While he hadn't said it outright, I came to understand that the campsite full of dilapidated gear constituted the entirety of his belongings, and he was living there for the summer. When he asked what I did for work, I felt too guilty and embarrassed to disclose the details of the salaried job that I'd just accepted; I just said that I was figuring it out. Candidly, he offered me encouragement and said he had confidence that I would.

By the time we got back to the campground, most of the other campers had left. I packed up my gear while Barry continued chatting, now with a bit more somber tone. I got the sense that the end of a weekend was tough on him too, albeit for different reasons than the requirement to return to an office on Monday morning. But I gave him my leftover food and beer before I left, which cheered him up. He didn't waste any time before cracking into one of the Kokanees.

We finished the day with ten fish (Barry's six to my four), two beers, and one frisbee—which came home with me. When we said our goodbyes, I took his number, promising to call him the next time I was around. I've yet to call, but I do look for Barry every time I'm on the Yak.

7
A VERY SPECIFIC CAST

Has something like this ever happened to you?

You're trying to make a very specific cast, and you try and try again, but you can't get it quite right. So, you give up for a moment on fishing and actually trying to catch a fish, and instead focus only on that very specific cast that you're trying to make.

In the end, you either make that very specific cast and feel pretty good about it, or you never make that very specific cast and you surrender; you give up, move on. But by moving on, you really just return to fishing, which is totally fine and great anyway, so your failure to make that very specific cast doesn't bother you very much.

But it *does* bother you, just a little.

Has that ever happened to you?

* * *

The turnoff to the one-lane dirt road was so overgrown that we nearly drove by it twice. Neither of us having been there before, it wasn't until the road opened up a couple hundred yards in that we got our first glimpses of the small pond. The calm water perfectly reflected the tall pines on the shoreline. I didn't feel like I was in the Pacific Northwest at all; the pond reminded me of those back home in Maine. My friend Richie, fresh off a flight from London and jetlagged, wasn't quite sure where he felt he was.

A few years prior, I heard there were trout in the pond and cataloged it as a place to fish during shoulder seasons, for a change of scenery, or perhaps when the rivers were blown out, as was the case that day. Richie and I had originally planned to go steelheading, but it rained for six consecutive days before he arrived, as it will often do when you plan your steelheading months in advance. We were disappointed but not terribly surprised. Still, we had decided that we were going fishing, somewhere, no matter what, so after studying weather forecasts, water flows, and calling a few friends, we finally decided to go to this little lake.

We launched the boat and drifted in silence, waiting for a fish to rise. Everywhere we looked, the pine tree reflections remained intact—not a trace of movement. Eventually, we chose a small cove to start in, for no other reason than the bow was already pointing in that direction. While I rowed slowly, Richie fished a single dry fly along the shoreline, next to structure, and along drop-offs.

Finally, we saw a rise under some overhanging tree limbs, nearly in casting distance. As I moved us within range, Richie started false casting. The fish rose again; he let it go, and we both watched as his fly landed in the branch that hung out above the water. His shoulders slumped, but from the rower's seat, I watched his mind work. Gently shaking his rod, the line waved in the air, the fly fell out of the tree, and landed not far from where the fish rose. The fish took it immediately. Richie set the hook and fought the rainbow to my waiting net.

Richie handed me the rod, and we switched seats. I began fishing in the same area, feeling confident, but nothing happened. After a while, we agreed to move on, but before we did, Richie suggested that I make a cast to the same spot where he had just caught his fish. I obliged, made my cast, and, unintentionally, landed the fly in that same overhanging limb. Wiggling the rod just like Richie had, the fly fluttered out of the tree and onto the water. Another fish rose and took it. As I steered it into the net, Richie and I locked eyes. Telepathically, we agreed that we must try this again.

But we could not repeat it; specifically, Richie was unable to cast into the tree. He made perfect cast after perfect cast onto the water, and pulled them all back, trying to put the fly into that same overhanging branch again. After some number of tries, he looked at me, shrugged, and we continued further down the bank.

* * *

Things like this sometimes happen while fishing: things that are not really fishing per se, but are more than fishing—the things we talk about and tell stories about when we come home from fishing.

Things like conversing without speaking; about where to row the boat, where to cast, when to switch seats, and when to move on.

Like catching a fish in the very same spot, in the very same way, as your friend did a moment before. Sure, that's really fishing, but I'm not talking about *how* it happened—I'm talking about *why* it happened.

Things like making a very specific cast into a tree (or trying to) because you did before or because your friend did.

Like refusing to *not* go fishing even though there are many, many other fine ways to spend time together.

Things like this happen because of fishing.

Do they happen to you? I'm sure they do.

8
PERFECTLY PACIFIC NORTHWEST

The light fades and the air goes still, matching the low, slack tide of the bay. The sounds of leaping coho, some far away, others eerily close, break the calm.

I watch my line slice through the water as I strip, when suddenly a small wake forms where I imagine the fly to be. I maintain the retrieve, and after two more strips it goes tight. I can feel the weight of the fish as I stretch the line and bury the hook. There's a brief pause as the fish gathers itself, and then the water explodes in a classic coho fight: spinning and cartwheeling as if a ceiling fan has landed in the water.

Bursts of laughter come from over my shoulder, and when I look, I can see Lucas landing a considerable fish of his own.

"*Wow*," he says, "It's a cutthroat."

"Are you sure?" I ask, skeptical. The irony isn't lost on me, however; I've just asked a fisheries biologist if he has correctly identified the trout in his hands.

"Yup," he replies, as much to himself as to me, his eyes fixed on the fish.

Lucas and I grew up in neighboring towns in mid-coast Maine, but went to different school districts. We met in high school while working together at the local fly shop. It was the first time we'd had an equally enthused and similarly-aged companion to fish with. Paul, our manager, fueled our fire when he introduced us to smallmouth bass and poppers. Until that point, our fly fishing had been limited to cold waters, and native brook trout and salmon. It wasn't easy, and we were often skunked. But Paul's smallie pond provided something new, exciting, and productive. That summer, we stashed an old canoe in the woods along the shoreline, and fished together after work on most days, coming to be known as "The Basstards."

A couple decades have passed. Though our fishing desires have changed a bit and the "pond" has morphed a number of times, Lucas and I are still close. Separately, we've lived in a couple dozen zip codes since leaving home, but we've fished our way around the South Island of New Zealand and across the West together.

In the twilight, the alleged cutthroat shoots out of his hand. We reel in and make for the beach, where our cooler and camp chairs await beside a stack of driftwood.

The next morning, I awake to rain on the tent fly. Checking my watch, I see there's still time before the tide rolls in. As I lie there in half-sleep comfort, the rain comes down harder, then gradually eases off. I can hear Lucas stirring in his tent. Stepping out of mine, I take in the surroundings. Calm morning mist hovers. Light rain dots the bay. A coho jumps on the horizon, its splash reaching my ears a second later.

Perfectly Pacific Northwest.

PART II
THERE

TRAVELING TO FLY FISH AND FLY FISHING WHILE TRAVELING

9
A PROPER TAKER

Fourteen days, four countries, three seasons.

One Atlantic salmon.

Before I landed one, I lost one. I saw it in the middle of the river, four feet out of the water, and in my bulging eyes, it looked as long as my leg and as big around as my thigh. My brain registered that it was a good one, and I wanted to land it badly. I might've been pulling too hard when the fly came out; who knows? All I know is that I wish I'd done something differently.

I can't remember ever feeling that level of physical ache after losing a fish. My body buzzed like I'd slammed my finger in a car door while looking the other way. At the same time, I was awestruck by the encounter, like arriving at my own surprise party. And, even though I'd lost it, I felt somehow relieved: one of these fish actually took my fly, so I must've been doing something right. Or maybe I'd just finally placed a fly in front of one that actually wanted to take it; a "proper taker" as Tomas, our ghillie on the River Tay, had put it a few months prior.

The day we fished with Tomas was our last of six in Scotland. By that time, we were going crazy. We'd tried everything we could think of—big flies, small flies, micro flies, bright flies, dull flies, flash flies, dry lines, long lines, sinking lines, fast swings, slow swings, stripped swings, fishing at dawn, fishing at dusk, fishing from dawn until dusk. We poured whisky down the river and down our gullets. We changed hats, then bought new ones. We changed beats, then changed rivers, then changed drainages. Alas. Four anglers, five days, and not a single take.

Fairly slow fishing.

When we arrived at Tomas' fishing hut, he was standing outside smoking a hand-rolled cigarette, staring at the river. Smoke swirled around his head signifying all the fishing thoughts he was having. I eyed him suspiciously as we approached, seeing as we were placing our faith in him for our final day. He looked like one of the nihilists from *The Big Lebowski*: like he'd just stepped out of some sort of biker bar rave party, covered in form-fitting, black leather accessorized with various buckles, webbing straps, patches, pins, and embroidery. I'd been forewarned that he was a peculiar fellow and hard to follow, partly due to his accent—which was a mix of eastern European and rural, Scottish dialects—and partly due to the quantity and rate at which he emitted his accented words.

We startled him when we entered his line of sight. With the butt of his smoldering cigarette between his lips, he quickly rolled another one by pulling tobacco from a rusted Altoids tin, all the while filling us in on the previous day's fishing. In doing so, he introduced us to the "proper taker."

Proper takers are anadromous fish fresh from the ocean. On the move, active, and aggressive, it doesn't matter what fly you cast or how you fish it, Tomas told us, a proper taker would take it. He'd hooked proper takers all over his beat and the pool we were looking at. *Here*, he pointed; over *there*, up here, down there. He'd caught proper takers on classics, dries, and tubes; sink tips and no-tips. He'd had five fish days, even ten fish days. Just yesterday, his sports—who had never fished before, of course—caught three proper takers before lunch, then went home for tea and a nap.

What I love about Tomas' phrase "proper taker" is that it acknowledges that the sentiment or opinion of the fish is a large factor in the likelihood of getting them to take a fly. In this sense, having an anadromous fish take a fly is more like an agreement or compromise between the angler and quarry as opposed to the tricking of prey by a predator. The philosophy of swinging flies for anadromous fish is based mainly on this concept. It also makes for a handy excuse when getting skunked, that being, "The fish weren't happy." Never mind the question of whether or not our own heads were in the right place.

We did not encounter any proper takers while fishing with Tomas. That made it six days in Scotland without a fish, plus the one day in England before we headed north, plus three I'd had in eastern Canada the previous fall. After dropping off half our party in Glasgow, the remaining two of us even talked ourselves into booking another day in Wales before I flew home. We figured if we were going to be skunked, we might as well go into debt, too.

I'd heard of a few blank streaks like ours before, but it had never happened to me. After investing that much time, mental capacity, and money into catching a specific fish, when you don't, the logical question becomes, "Was it worth it?" I have thought long about this, and while I do believe the answer is yes, if I'm being honest, it takes some self-convincing. And in such an exercise, you also realize, perhaps for the first time, that there's a limit to the extent to which you'll go. You may or may not be close to it, but you at least acknowledge that the limit exists.

I ate lunch with my distant cousin Louanne in London before flying home and told her about my fishing trip. After clarifying the details—international flight, car and house rentals, private water bookings, eight days, no fish, etc.—she mulled it over in her head for a moment, then burst out laughing.

"I can't wait to tell my friends this story," she said.

I was thinking the same thing, but was mostly sure that *my* friends would at least be laughing *with* me.

While painful (emotionally), exhausting (physically), and also entirely unsustainable (financially), returning home skunked didn't deter me. Instead, I wanted to catch one even more. See, I was destined to fish for Atlantic salmon; it's in my blood. For decades before I was born, my paternal grandfather and his brother, neither of whom I ever met, fished for Atlantic salmon in eastern Canada and Maine. Their boot prints and wisdom are in those rivers, and I knew that, with their help, I'd find the fish I was looking for. So, two months after I returned from Scotland, five of us made our own trip to New Brunswick to fish the famed Miramichi River.

We were on the front end of the summer run, but that was intentional. The majority of the salmon would come after we were gone, but whatever fish we *did* encounter would be right out of the Atlantic and, presumably, ready to take flies properly. After my experience in Scotland, I was more than happy to trade good numbers of stale fish for low numbers of proper takers. All I wanted was one. (Maybe two. And one for each of my buddies, of course.)

As non-residents, we were required by law to fish with guides in New Brunswick, and they met us at our cabin as we unloaded our gear. We all exchanged pleasantries, and it immediately became clear that they were equally as eccentric as Tomas, albeit in their own ways. Thick eastern Canadian drawls colored their endless supply of stories, unique slang, and bone-dry humor.

They had us in stitches in no time, though it was hard to tell what was in jest and what wasn't. In response to someone saying that they were from 'out West,' one of the guides clarified by asking, "Where's that, like, Massachusetts?" I'm still not sure if that was a joke or not.

To confirm a question or acknowledge an opinion, they always responded with an inhalation-response: "Hhhyaa."

In the evening of our first day, I stepped into Bridge Pool. It's an easy wade, fished from river-right and, as you might guess, is in plain sight of a bridge. A small, gravel bar island upstream of the run forms a long slick below, like a giant acute triangle, with definitive seams on both sides, and it's easy to see that it's a perfect traveling lane.

The fish that I lost took an Undertaker right in the middle of the triangle. In a boil of water, it was hooked instantly. My rod buckled, and the reel spun so fast that it shook. White-knuckling the cork, I could feel the thick Scandi shooting head cutting through the water as the fish surged across the river. Then, the tension released, and I saw the fish break the surface. It landed in a crash, and to my amazement, I was still tight to it.

Eventually, the fish tired. With my guide Ian in position with the net and the fish twenty feet away, the fly flew out. We looked at each other, mouths open, both of us unsure what to say. It wasn't meant to be. But, as every fishing story goes (so long as you make it long enough), eventually, the fish is caught. That, or you die, I guess.

On our way back to the cabin, while recalling the encounter, I remarked that I thought I'd seen a fish roll before hooking the fish that I lost. Danny, another one of the guides, just nodded. "That's why I always watch the water," he said, "because you can see things." I'm mostly sure he was serious that time.

In the morning session of our last day in New Brunswick, my fourteenth day of Atlantic salmon fishing, I hooked another proper one in Bridge Pool. In similar fashion to the one I lost, the fish took the fly in a swirl and immediately sprinted downstream. It didn't stop until after the backing knot was far out of my rod tip. By that time, Tyler, my guide for the day, was standing next to me.

"He ripped ya," he said, as much in observation as anything. I couldn't muster any coherent response.

And then it was in the net.

Its colors were marine, oceanic. A belly and sides of bright whites and silvers, outside of any standard color spectrums, transitioned into a metallic, oyster shell gray back. In between were clusters of black spots, no two alike. Fins with tips so clear that you could read a newspaper through them, as a good friend says. Its head, threatening. Nose and jaw, pointed. Eyes piercing, irritated that its migration had been interrupted.

It was everything I had wished for and fished for, yet more. Beyond adequate, perfectly fitting, and just right. Proper.

10
BIIRU KUDASAI

It was an odd combination of déjà vu and stress dream. I'd been here before, but this time something different was preventing me from completing the task at hand.

In Tokyo for business, a weekend off granted me the opportunity for some angling. Specifically, I'd be night fishing for seabass in Yokohama harbor, south of the capital. After spending the week in all-day meetings helmed by translators and reminiscent of Bill Murray in *Lost in Translation*, fueled on black tea, white rice, and numerous colors of raw fish, it was approaching midnight on Friday. We were to launch at 12:30 am, and the only remaining task was to acquire provisions.

Now, I stood in a Japanese convenience store, trying to choose a selection of food and drink to sustain me for the evening's fishing. All while my host and the captain were waiting.

I was more than familiar with the procedure. I've been successfully executing pre-fishing trip gas station shopping missions for years. My choices are generally the same: peppered beef jerky for protein, Clif Bars for calories, Sour Patch Watermelons for my sweet tooth, orange juice for scurvy, coffee for caffeine, and beer…for having beer.

These are easy pickups at any 7-Eleven, Circle K, or Stinker Store, but tonight I was walking in circles with nothing to show for it.

I decided to start with something straightforward: coffee. Grabbing a paper cup, I approached a line of four likely-looking machines. Eyeing them, I pushed one of several buttons with pictures of steaming cups and waited for something to happen. Suddenly, hot water started spewing out of the machine and onto the floor. Across the aisle, another patron muttered something at me in Japanese.

My host, Daisuke, appeared.

"What are you doing?!"

"Making coffee?"

"That's the coffee," he said, pointing to a nearly identical apparatus. "I'll make it. Get your food. And hurry up!"

So I went for food, really feeling the pressure of holding up the entire enterprise, and located what looked like candy bars. Shiny packages glistened in the fluorescent lights. Eventually, I found one I could interpret: *CHOCOLATE*, it read, in capital letters. It felt segmented, like a Caramello. I grabbed two.

I wanted something salty, too, so I stared at bags of chip-like items and picked up two to investigate further. As I'd done every day since arriving, I wished I could read Japanese. Blue bag or red bag? I was in *The Matrix*.

Finally, I brought my grub selections to the counter where Daisuke was waiting with the coffee. He looked at me, still grinning.

"I've never had those," he said, nodding at the chips. That wasn't the reaction I'd hoped for.

The cashier rang everything up, then pointed at the screen showing the total. I inspected the bills in my wallet and attempted to do math while Daisuke stood in the doorway looking back at me. Meanwhile, a line had formed. With a shaking hand, I held out a credit card. The cashier studied it, looked at me, then ran it. The register slowly processed the foreign plastic. Sweat beaded on my forehead. The cashier looked at me again, then back at the cash register. Daisuke looked at me. Everyone in the store looked at me.

Finally, the register chirped. Relieved, I scribbled my name and bolted.

At the dock, we boarded quickly. We had a twenty-minute run, so I grabbed a candy bar and took a bite. It was dry as cinnamon and had the consistency of raw mushrooms. I put the rest back and grabbed the chips, or at least what I hoped were chips. I ripped open the bag and studied them. Daisuke came up to me, chuckling.

"Let me try one of those." He threw one in his mouth, and frowned.

"These are terrible!" he said, and dumped the rest over the gunwale.

The engine opened, and we were off.

Reaching our first spot, we started stringing rods while our captain pulled out his fly boxes. I was eager to see his selection, anticipating an array of patterns as different from my own as the snacks I'd just puzzled over. But he handed me a slight variation of a Clouser, and I could only laugh. The fish that ate it wasn't laughing, though; it easily recognized its food.

I admired my first Japanese sea bass, which looked like a cross between a striper and a snook, and then sent it back into the harbor.

Daisuke reached into the cooler and grabbed two cans that needed no translation whatsoever.

"Welcome to Japan, Jesse-san."

11
THE TEN-THOUSANDTH CAST

Long before I ever went fishing for them, I was told that muskies were the fish of a thousand casts or even *ten* thousand casts. The fact that there was a difference of a factor of ten between these figures immediately made me discredit the estimates, but also wasn't entirely surprising. Even when prefaced with phrases like "Trust me, I measured," or "Believe me, I counted," or perhaps even "Now, you know I never exaggerate," I am always incredulous towards statistics uttered by anyone who fishes. In fact, caveats such as these only increase my suspicion, certainly in the figures that follow and possibly in the individual who shares them.

Nevertheless, there are only so many ways to express magnitude, and in the case of catching a musky, I *did* accept the fact that they were very difficult to catch.

Yet in planning my first trip to fish for musky, I couldn't help but feel like I had a leg up. At the time, most of the fishing I'd been doing was for steelhead—well-known, perhaps even before musky, as a fish of a thousand casts. The mental exertion of casting all day, or all trip even, for a single fish wasn't novel to me. The patience, persistence, and focus required in steelheading would be very similar to that required while musky fishing, I assumed.

The other thing I knew beforehand about fishing for musky was that *slack is evil*. I knew this because it was printed in bold, sinister, capital letters on a bumper sticker given to me before the trip by my coworker Jerry. The bumper sticker was from the Hayward Fly Fishing Company in Hayward, Wisconsin, a fly shop specializing in fly fishing for musky. Jerry grew up near there, and had spent many days fishing for musky in the area. He stressed to me the importance of minimizing—or better yet, eliminating—slack in the system (excess, unnecessary fly line between the fly and the hand holding the line) as an antidote to weak or missed hooksets. Jerry also said that a strip set was necessary when a musky took the fly, and a *hard* one at that, because it takes a lot of force to sink the large hooks into their big, tough mouths. The less slack in the system, the better the strip set, and the lesser the chances of botching the hookup.

Another coworker, Paul, and I went to Wisconsin to fish with our friend Dave, who lives in the northern part of the state. A gracious host, Dave picked the dates and planned the itinerary. We'd booked our flights accordingly, landing in Minneapolis and then immediately made our way northeast to meet Dave. I'd never been to Wisconsin before but grew up in a similar latitude in Maine, so the surroundings felt eerily like home to me, even though the business names on gas stations and supermarkets were unfamiliar.

It was the middle of October, and the countryside looked a bit bleak, as if the only thing separating us from winter was a few feet of snow. But we were planning on cold weather—actually hoping for it, for the fishing's sake—and had packed accordingly. Still, it's a different climate in the Midwest than in the Pacific Northwest, where I'd been doing my steelheading; a 'different cold.' A forty-five-degree day with constant drizzle in the Northwest may feel tropical compared to forty-five degrees with a stiff breeze in the Midwest, or it may feel like putting your entire body in a frozen cocktail, depending on which way you're traveling.

The first day, on our way to the river with Dave's drift boat in tow, we stopped at a rural gas station to fill up. I went inside to inspect the local convenience store cuisine and was immediately taken by the melted cheese dispenser. Of course, I'd heard of Cheeseheads, but I didn't realize just how literal the term was, nor how liberal their application of cheese. I elected to forgo the bulk purchase and instead acquired a large bag of cheese curds; "for sharing," I told myself.

Walking back to the truck, I observed a conversation taking place between Dave, Paul, and another gentleman. They were all leaning on the gunwales of the trailered drift boat when I arrived, and, listening for a moment, I realized that the other guy, an old-time local, had never seen one before. At first, I found this detail amusing, but after we said goodbye to him and started making our way to the river, I couldn't help but wonder if it was *us* who somehow weren't in the know. My doubts went away when we reached boat launch and saw the exact same drift boat on the trailer pulled by the friends that we were going to fish with. One of those, the owner of the boat, was a fishing mentor of Dave's, further cementing the fact that we were in good shape.

Getting my first look at the river, my thoughts quickly turned from cheese curds and drift boats to musky. Dave handed me a rigged fly rod and I inspected it. On the business end was a thirteen-inch bucktail fly tied hollow-style. It was nearly as long and as wide as my forearm and was tied to an equally long piece of knottable wire. I wondered if dispensing melted cheese on the fly would make it more or less attractive to a musky.

We dropped the boats in the water and began our fishing day, the first of four. Our friends in the other boat pushed downstream, leaving us a few hundred yards of the left bank and a big eddy that had produced fish in the past. For some reason, I was given the bow, and as we approached, I tried to recall as much as I could about musky fishing. *Slack is evil. Strip set hard.*

Following Dave's instructions, I started fishing as soon as we were in casting distance of the bank, dropping casts as close as I could. My official count of casts had begun, but I'd overlooked one critical detail: the *type* of cast that I'd be making a thousand or ten thousand times. What I quickly learned was that casting a size eight classic wet fly with a 400-grain Scandinavian-style shooting head on a thirteen-foot Spey rod for steelhead is extremely different from casting a foot-long 6/0 fish pattern (not to be confused with a *baitfish* pattern) with a 400-grain integrated shooting head on an eleven-weight single-hand rod for musky. They're about as different as the rivers that the two fish live in: one, glacial green-blue, steep, swift, and rumbling; the other, tannin brown-black, gradual, unhurried, and hushed.

Casting a musky setup like that is chore enough, especially if you've never done it before. But with some minor technique adjustments, the process becomes much more efficient and less labor-intensive. Utilizing a combination of Belgian-style casts, water loads, double hauls, and learning to resist the urge to apply as much muscle as I could, I was able to get into a comfortable casting rhythm, casting my fly up to seventy feet or so, over and over again. But simply launching the fly out to seventy feet is one thing; the real skill comes when trying to place that same fly within a few inches of a dynamic river bank over and over again, first at sixty-eight feet, then sixty-four, then seventy-three, then fifty-eight, as you float downstream. It's easy to convince yourself that close enough is good enough, but when your host and veteran musky angler is repeatedly telling you, "Closer to the bank next time," you start to realize that there's a specific reason, and it's not for them to hear their own voice.

Dave offered small critiques to my retrieves as we neared the eddy slowly. Once in range, he gave instructions on how to fish the spot, dividing the upstream-flowing water into quarters. Laying down my first cast in the eddy, I thought that it looked like a really fishy spot, but then quickly reminded myself that I didn't know anything first-hand about musky or musky fishing. I made another cast, started working the fly back to the boat, and watched as it slithered, pulsed, and kicked underwater.

Of the many challenges that come with fishing for fish of some-thousand casts is that you don't know which of the some-thousand casts you're about to make. You don't know when that one fish you're looking for is going to take your fly. We maximize our odds by putting our fly in the best water for the most amount of time, but the fact remains that for fish of some-thousand casts, any cast can hook one. So, the challenge then lies in fishing each and every cast as if your fly is going to swim in front of a fish. As it was, my thirtieth cast turned out to be the ten-thousandth.

The musky came out from the undercut bank and swallowed the giant white fly in its alligator jaws. The fly, as big and bold as it was in the dark water, simply disappeared. A flash of honey-gold in the water told us that the fish had turned and was headed back for the undercut.

Dave yelled something, and while I tried to listen, all I could hear was, "*Slack is evil. Strip set hard.*" So, I did what I heard, and pulled the line tight. When it didn't come as tight as I thought it would, my in-the-moment reaction was to think that the fish was coming toward the boat. I strip set again, and again, hoping to eliminate all that evil slack and also embed the big hook into that big musky's big mouth. It seemed like the fish was still coming at the boat, so for good measure, I leaned back in my seat and lifted the rod while continuing to strip set hard. It was too much: too much pressure on a too-flexed rod that was attached to a too-big fish. Something had to give, and it wasn't going to be the musky. The rod exploded, and the leader broke. The fish was gone.

As I comprehended the events that had just transpired, my mind eventually settled on the fact that I was now, without a doubt, starting ten thousand casts over from the beginning. My one opportunity at one fish for the trip just happened to have come in the first ten minutes of the first day. And…there it went. I swallowed these details about as well as I would've swallowed that big, white musky fly covered in dispensed liquid cheese.

Judging by the fact that I didn't hook another musky that trip, I guess I didn't make it back up to ten thousand casts. Actually, I don't need to "guess." I know, because I counted.

Trust me.

12
SWIMMERS

At the end of the day, when I make my first step onto the dock, it'll feel like I'm still on the boat. By then, my body will be tuned to the swell, my hips, knees, and ankles rocking, bending, and adjusting naturally to the rhythm of the waves. That first step is disorienting—the ground seems to be moving, but I know it's not—yet it's also satisfying to think that I've been on the water so long that it's now my equilibrium, my baseline. Until then, I'm still finding my sea legs.

For the moment, I'm standing on the casting platform. My toes, spread wide apart, are grabbing and gripping this SeaDek for all their worth, which, evidently, isn't much. Thankfully, this isn't my first time, and muscle memory is starting to take over, slowly making the act of balancing on the platform an unconscious one. Behind me, holding the skiff in place from the poling platform, is Andy—an old friend and one of my best, who, lucky for me, also happens to be a tarpon fishing guide. In front of us spreads an expansive flat, a golden-tan bottom clearly visible through the slight chop. Beyond that, a maze of mangrove islands, each unique and yet, to the tourist angler (me), startlingly similar and completely disorienting. The horizon line, mangrove green, splits the two blues of sky and sea. Here, silently, with eyes wide open, we wait for an intersection with 'swimmers'—migrating adult tarpon, coming right at us.

With us in the skiff are two other anglers: Bre and Wilds. They're new friends to me, but old friends of Andy's. We three have intersected because of this mutual friend and are now in the process of forming a connection of our own; a friendship and shared memories to take home. The boat is at physical capacity, but as we chat and get to know each other, it seems like fewer of us would make for much less of an experience. Our personalities are like the flies stuck into the carpet under the gunwale: of varied form, with unique paths, yet all bringing unique and incremental elements.

When we arrived at this flat, the tide was slack and we couldn't yet see through the glare—antithetical conditions for fishing for swimmers. While we all kept one eye on the flat, we killed time, discussing and debating matters as profound as creation and evolution, as practical as business and politics, and as elementary as various gummy candies and fast foods. We waited for what seemed like a long time, but that was by design. In most fishing situations, if you aren't early, you're late.

I love it when worlds collide, but I'm more often on the colliding side of the event. Now, I'm doing my best to embrace the moment, listen more than I talk, and let it happen…all while trying not to make a fool of myself. If our mutual acquaintance believed so strongly that Bre, Wilds, and I should meet, then I should have faith in him that we will indeed get along well. It occurs to me that our encounters with the tarpon are not dissimilar. With faith in our guide, we make the connection we seek, enjoy it as it happens, and learn while doing it. There's no guarantee you won't make a fool of yourself along the way, but a good guide (or good friend) won't care anyway.

It's now mid-morning and the sun's high enough that the glare is all-but-gone. I can feel the temperature rising quickly. Living in the country's northern third makes me much less accustomed to this degree of heat and humidity, but I recall something another tarpon guide said to me once: "It doesn't get good until you're sweating." As an angler, I'm what you might call a fair-weather superstitionist—happy to buy into any colloquialism, adage, or cliché *if* it appears to improve my fishing in the moment. So, as a single bead of sweat forms and slowly makes its way down my forehead, I wipe it off and think, 'We should see one any second.'

Fly fishing for tarpon might as well be a myth. Explaining it is an exercise in irrationality and a test of vocabulary. There's just one too many absurd elements to it: giant fish, shallow water, small fly, light tippet. Fishing for swimmers takes the pursuit to another level. We just wait here, in our little boat, and let them come to us. That's a gross oversimplification of the mission, but in concept, it holds. What a world; what a way to fish.

We all know that the blind squirrel occasionally finds the nut, but we might also say that the acorn sometimes lands on the blind squirrel's head. Such is the case with swimmers. They can be intercepted solely by chance or coincidence, though I don't recommend that as a primary tactic. Adding some knowledge and experience to the pursuit is preferred, with the ideal scenario including a degree of confidence as well. A good guide brings all three, and the more eyes on the water, the better.

"OK, I've got some coming at…" Andy says.

I see them before he finishes the sentence. There are three, and I point my rod.

"…ten o'clock. Yup, you got 'em. Here we go."

I feel Bre and Wilds adjust to get their own glimpses, followed by a combination of garbled phrases of amazement. It happens to be my turn on the bow, but the shot I'm about to take is for all of us.

Swimming high in the water column, their green-gray bodies starkly contrast with the sandy bottom in the translucent, aquamarine water. The chop on the water sporadically distorts their image, as though time skips ahead with each small wave. The fish jump from 150 feet away, to 125, to 110, to 95.

There they are and here I am. That we meet at all is a gift to me from both my friend on the poling platform and the tarpon themselves. I try to remember this and be happy enough just to see them, but that feeling comes and goes as quickly as I think it. Now, I want more: I want to hook one and, dare I say it, land it. I start false casting immediately because, again, it's either early or late.

Trial and error and learning by making mistakes are the best methods for figuring out how to feed tarpon, swimmers especially. The trick is simply to know what to do. For me, knowing what to do is more a function of knowing what *not* to do than performing any well-defined task. I'm fortunate enough to have done it wrong so many times that, at this point, there's little else left to do but do it right.

The sum of all I've read, been told, and experienced advises me that the ideal presentation is a delicate combination of placing the fly far enough in front of the fish so that they can come upon it seemingly of their own means, yet close enough so that they don't regard it as too out of the way and keep swimming right by. These distances—"far enough" and "close enough"—aren't constants and can really only be estimated; they are functions of variables such as the depth of the fish, how fast it's traveling, and water clarity, plus the angler's or guide's opinions and risk tolerance.

This assumes that the fish are swimming more or less directly at the boat, which is undoubtedly possible, though most often not the case. As such, angles of presentation become increasingly important. Unfortunately, the angler doesn't get to pick theirs; the boat remains in a relatively fixed position while the tarpon swim wherever they swim. A great angle of presentation moves the fly mostly-away from the fish, as real prey presumably would react if suddenly in the presence of a predator twenty or so times its size, and I've heard it said that the less-away from the fish the presentation, the less likely it is to get eaten. I agree with this, generally speaking, but anomalies outside of this rule are about as common as cocktails after fishing. I've found that the presentation that gets an eat is the best one.

Getting the fly to the right place is essential, but still second to how it moves once it's there. With swimmers, fly retrieval is an ultimate balance of not-too-much and just-enough. They need to be able to take the fly with relative ease, but it can't be too easy—or too hard. If I move the fly too fast, they'll disregard it completely. They want to overtake it in the water, as if they're winning a race. As the angler moving the fly, I'm trying to rig the race so the tarpon can't lose.

By now, I've watched these three swimmers long enough to have a good sense of their course, and I've false casted enough times that I can let the line go any time and get in the game. Suddenly, time skips ahead again. The fish are now almost at nine o'clock.

"Lay it down!" I can tell by Andy's tone that it's gone from early to late.

Hastily, I make a final haul and shoot fly line into the ether. The fly lands past the lead fish by fifteen feet, meaning my fly line is right in its face.

I hear a sharp inhale through teeth behind me, an audible cringe. The tarpon immediately doglegs away from the fly and sinks to the bottom while swimming past us. The two fish behind follow suit. I stop stripping the fly; the boat is quiet. I've blown the shot and made a fool of myself, but everyone knows that I know it, so nothing needs to be said.

I mutter to myself, and instantly, unwillingly, my mind begins to replay the events. Thankfully, before I get lost in what just happened, the daydream is interrupted.

"Get ready," Andy says. "Here's another one. A solo."

It's swimming straight at the bow, impossible to miss. I point my rod at the fish, signifying that the target is acquired, but only for a moment, and then I'm in my back cast. The skiff swings ever-so-slightly clockwise, setting me up for an ideal eleven o'clock shot.

"It's all yours."

This time, I make sure that I'm early. The fly, followed by a leader and seventy feet of fly line, lands in a straight line that perfectly matches this swimming solo's path.

Andy: "Beautiful!"

Bre: "Ooh, nice."

Wilds: "Great shot!"

The encouragement gives me confidence, and now I'm fishing without thinking. Instead of skipping ahead, time now slows.

I see my fly in the water, and I sense that the tarpon does too. I start stripping. Immediately, the fish reacts, adjusts slightly to track the fly, and gains speed just below the surface. I maintain the strip and watch as a catcher's-mitt-sized mouth opens, half out of the water. The fly vanishes.

A second passes before I understand that this tarpon and I have officially intersected. I sink the barb and seal the connection.

In another second, the line clears and the spinning reel serenades us. The tarpon jumps along the mangrove horizon line in the distance—everything stops, briefly—then lands, and we remain connected. The whole boat cheers. I turn and meet their smiles with my own. Our connection is now sealed.

It seems that we are back to where we started. Me on the bow, pointing my rod, watching as the swimmer swims, trying to keep my balance.

13
FLY-IN

They gave me the shotgun seat because I was the youngest. Settling into the cockpit of the float plane, I buckled up and took in my surroundings. Countless dials, levers, switches, lights, wires, and small windows encapsulated me. Each and every one looked straightforward yet disastrous if pushed, pulled, or turned at the wrong moment or in the wrong way. Most of the labels and placards were faded if not worn away completely; the several handwritten replacements and additions ("Water rudders up!" "DOORS & WINDOWS," and "Is everybody in?") certainly added some character, but I wasn't sure if 'character' was an attribute I looked for in a plane.

Lower on the dashboard was a cubby space that appeared to store odds and ends. In it, I could see a couple of pencils, a mini wire-bound notebook, and a rolled-up magazine. Without thinking much about it, I grabbed the end of the magazine and slid it halfway out of the cubby to inspect. On the cover, peering back at me was a naked woman posing, small stars covering her breasts. I immediately shoved the magazine back into its place, but it was too late. I heard laughter from the seat behind me.

"Whatcha got there, young man?"

It was 'Uncle' John. I knew he was joking around—he's always joking around—yet for some reason, I still felt embarrassed.

Uncle John, my (actual) Uncle Frank, my father, and I were finally taking off for the last leg of our journey to the lakefront tent camp where we'd be staying for the next week. After three full days of land travel involving a border crossing, a car ferry, highways, state routes, dirt roads, and finally a train ride into Schefferville, the nearly-abandoned logging and mining town in northern Quebec, a stubborn rain shower had delayed us for an additional two hours. Everyone's patience was being tested.

At fifteen, this was my first destination fishing trip, and I was ripe with all of the elements I'd later come to know as savory side dishes to the whole experience: anticipations, nerves, hopes, over-preparations, expectations, and unknowns.

Finally, the pilot climbed in. He was tall, thin, and didn't look much older than some of the seniors on my high school football team.

"Buckle up, boys," he instructed. "Let's get the hell out of here before the weather gets any worse, eh?"

Then, as if performing a solo on some massive mechanical instrument, he played the dials, levers, and switches of the cockpit. His hands ran up, down, and across as he pressed, turned, and flipped, the end result being that the engine sputtered, fired, and the propeller spun to life.

"Catch all that?" he asked, looking at me and grinning.

The engine found its rhythm and smoothed out. Stepping out of the cockpit, the pilot untied the dock lines and tossed them. Then he simultaneously pushed off the dock while stepping back onto the plane's float, an impressively graceful move which also served to angle the plane ever so slightly. We now faced the length of the lake, the wind in our face. He stretched his neck, cracked his knuckles, then grabbed the radio piece and called in our departure.

Pushing on the throttle, the engine roared and we all fell back in our seats. The plane lurched forward and we began our takeoff, heading down the lake. Gaining speed as we went, every fourth or fifth wave crashed into the front of the floats, bouncing us as we went until we finally came on plane. Now gaining speed quickly, what a moment ago seemed unlikely now seemed inevitable. As if a cork popped from a wine bottle, the lake released us, and we were airborne. We banked clockwise, circling back over the lake, and then we were flying over the northern Quebec taiga.

* * *

In many ways, our trip began a year prior as the idea took form. From then on, I'd eavesdropped on countless phone calls between my father, John, and Frank leading up to it, and the outlook seemed to hinge on whatever fishing report or prediction they'd just received. Each phone call ended the same way, though—optimistically and enthusiastically—and the mood was infectious.

At the time, I was a dishwasher at a local restaurant. One of the chefs there was also a fly angler, and when he learned about our trip, he immediately said he would tie us some flies to bring along. I gave him a copy of the suggested patterns list, and a few weeks later, he presented me with a fly box filled with an assortment of masterfully-tied Lee Wulff dry fly patterns. It was a gift unlike any other I'd received; the first time anyone had tied flies for me, and clear that he'd spent a considerable amount of time for my sake. The gift was also incredibly practical, as I'd use the flies as soon as I arrived. I showed them to my father when I got home, and the fact that he culled several for his own fly box confirmed that they were great ties.

Our destination was another large lake, where our camp host, chef, and guide (all the same person) awaited us. The camp was on the lake, but we planned to fish the several small rivers that flowed into the lake and the bigger one that flowed out of it. The latter held the most intrigue for us. For months, we'd been reading stories and dreaming about the large brook trout that resided in it and happily ate dry flies.

Countless ponds, lakes, bogs, swamps, and meandering brooks, streams, and rivers passed underneath as we flew. An infinite network of game trails ran amongst them. Seemingly chaotic, the trails were like veins and arteries, merging, braiding, and splitting over and over again. I was thinking about deer and moose and coyotes when all of a sudden, a giant herd of caribou appeared. It was the first time I'd seen them in person, and even though I subconsciously knew what they were, it took a second to register and an acknowledgement from our pilot to confirm.

Eventually, the pilot changed our course slightly, signifying that our destination was near. He pointed out of the cockpit at one particular lake and then gave us a thumbs up, which we returned. I could make out several tents near a sandy beach and a wooden dock below us. Losing elevation, we again did a semi-circle and squared up to the length of the lake for our landing. Approaching the surface of the lake, the engine slowed—almost paused—and we gently alighted. As soon as we touched down, the pilot launched into another routine of dials and levers.

I looked at my father, and he beamed at me, patting my shoulder. He and I had been in float planes together before, had flown into some remote ponds, and had shared plenty of adventures, but this was something entirely different and special for both of us. As a child, you're at the mercy of your parents or elders for your recreation. They mostly decide where you're going and what you do there. At some point, you begin to express your opinions and desires on where and what, but it's still up to them to make it happen until eventually you're old enough to be a critical part of a trip, ready and qualified to contribute and pull your own weight, as the saying goes. This was the first time that my father and I were going fishing together in a place neither of us had been before. It was tough to say who was more excited to finally arrive.

Waiting at the dock was our host for the week, Martin. He introduced himself, shook our hands, and helped unload our gear. Martin and the pilot obviously knew each other well, and they seemed to speak their own language. In the few minutes that the plane was at the dock, the two efficiently exchanged pertinent information on weather, water, arrivals and departures of various clients, and a few inside jokes. Then, double-checking that we had all our gear, the pilot climbed back in and started the engine.

"Have fun, boys," he yelled. "Maybe I'll see you for dinner in a few days, eh?"

Settling into camp, we peppered Martin with questions. He was used to the drill, patiently answering all our inquiries. He was vague in his responses, though, revealing just enough facts to make himself believable while curbing our optimism at the same time. On a fundamental level, this—managing expectations—is probably the most effective way to ensure a successful destination fishing trip (that and keeping guests safe from injury). Piecing together answers from Martin, we realized that the fishing had been tough as of late. An abnormally dry and hot summer made for low and warm water, which in turn had pushed the brook trout into a few deeper pools. That, or they chose to remain in the lake itself. It was less than ideal, but what could we do?

This is, I quickly learned, the crux of destination fishing trips: you're only there when you can make it, and you can't control the conditions when you do arrive. It's like an algebra equation with one too many variables. Whether it all adds up to good fishing is simply beyond the predictive power of the mathematician.

Hence, the strategy for choosing dates for a destination trip is a subtle yet complex affair. You can aim for the "best" time to be there, but this is a moving target, subject to change, and typically already booked anyway. Early-season can be great, showing your flies to hungry fish that haven't seen any in a while. But if you show up "too early" (something also out of your control), the fish may not be interested in eating, or they may not even be there at all. Late-season certainly decreases the chances of crowds, but have the fish come and gone? Have they seen every fly in your box already? Choosing dates also assumes that calendars are open—yours, the guide's, outfitter's, and lodge's, that is.

In any case, I'm fairly certain that you don't want to get there after it has been good for a while because it can only get worse from there. I think the ideal scenario is to arrive just as it starts to get good. Which means, it could be very slow when you first show up.

* * *

There were several tents at our camp, the largest of which served as the guest sleeping quarters, kitchen, and dining room. The excitement was palpable inside as we unpacked and got organized. Also present were hordes of mosquitoes, which we had regrettably allowed to enter en masse as we brought in our gear. I'd been told that the bugs could be bad, but I stood in awe at just how many were inside the tent. In addition to the dozens hovering over our heads, we could see swarms in the unreachable ceiling corners of the tent. Uncle Frank suggested lighting a mosquito coil, and this was seconded by John, but vetoed by my father, citing the health concerns of inhaling fumes that were toxic enough to kill insects. The debate turned out to be moot because Martin, overhearing our discussion, informed us that the box of coils never made it onto the plane anyway.

Two bunk bed cots lined one side of the tent, and as I made for the top of one to lay out my sleeping bag, my father intervened.

"Let me take that one and sleep above John. He's going to snore loud enough to keep Martin awake in his own tent."

I looked at the second set of cot bunks. They were only a couple of feet away from the one John (and now my father) would be in. I acknowledged the gesture, but it didn't seem to me that it would make a difference. Looking at Frank, it appeared this just-revealed information about John's snoring was new to him as well, and he was having the same thoughts as me.

"I almost brought earplugs…" he said, trailing off.

It turned out John's snoring wasn't much of a problem that first night. After countless openings of the tent door over the course of our arrival, the mosquitoes were so thick inside and relentless in their bloodthirsty quest that no one slept well. I put on a head net in the middle of the night, and this brought relief from bites, but not from the sound of the swarm around my head. By the time morning had lightened the inside of the tent enough to see, we were already out of our sleeping bags.

Eventually, Martin entered our tent and prepared coffee and breakfast. We were anxious to get on the water—pacing around the tent, tapping on the dining table, opening and closing the door to look at the weather and stage gear. We must've been as annoying to Martin as the mosquitos had been to us. When he finally served us—nothing short of a bush-kitchen masterpiece—we were all so antsy that we hardly gave it a second glance as we wolfed it down.

Unintentionally, we had assumed the roles of fresh-off-the-plane clients, champing at the bit while the been-there-all-season staff attends to the necessary daily routines and duties. And despite such guests being ignorant of their behavior, it still creates an awkward environment. It's best to hold faith that the guide and staff know what they're doing and have the guests' best interests in mind. Their product is performance- and experience-based, after all. (Unless they actually don't know what they're doing, or have some masochistic tendencies, both of which aren't fully out of the question.)

I had this point reiterated to me years later with a Colorado guide buddy on his off-day. I'd flown in to fish for pike and, after spending the previous day running errands, I was antsy to get started. But on our way to the lake that morning, my friend stopped at a sit-down restaurant for breakfast, and my patience stretched. When our food finally arrived, I ate it in no more than two minutes.

"Did you even taste that?" he asked, with little effort to conceal his displeasure with my anxiousness.

I got the message, ordered another cup of coffee, and made sure to pay the check. That evening, after the sun fell below the mountains, I landed my only fish of the day. '*I told you so*' was not necessary.

In an effort to avoid the bugs surrounding the tent, my father began assembling his fly rod inside our tent. Then, with the rod leaning on the dining table from the floor, he began to string the guides. Although somewhat unorthodox, I didn't think anything of the procedure until I heard the unmistakable sound of a fly rod falling onto the floor. I winced and, upon hearing a string of expletives, knew there was a problem. I turned around and looked at my father, who was hunched over. The tip section of the rod that he was planning to fish all week was broken. The tent went quiet.

This was more than a broken fishing pole—it was a disruption and compromise to the plan. From a practical perspective, a fly rod is a tool that performs a specific task, and the owner knows how to wield it well. The piece of equipment, selected and fine-tuned for the task at hand, was now useless, and my father would have to resort to the back-up, a lesser alternative. To a degree, the blow was also emotional because there is something intangible in fishing with *your rod*. There's a connection that exists between it and you; it's an old friend that you know well, and when you can't fish with your friend, a valuable element is lost.

The mood lifted as finally, it was time to go fishing. We piled into one of Martin's big square stern canoes with all our gear and took off down the lake toward the outlet, the river for which we had chosen this location. As Martin had described to us earlier, the water was very low. But in our excitement, we'd already forgotten (or perhaps, had chosen to not remember) this detail. Approaching the outlet, it seemed like hardly any water was flowing out of the lake into the river. We all glanced at each other and made various this-doesn't-look-so-good faces. Martin spun the boat around and backed us into the shore so he could stand up in the stern and avoid the numerous barely-submerged boulders. We unloaded the boat and started hiking down the outlet.

* * *

After nearly a year of planning to make it happen, then days of travel to get there, it was almost too much. The tension was ripe. We started following a rough trail alongside the outlet. Downstream, we could see the river splitting around a small island.

"Jesse, why don't you fish that side channel," Martin said, pointing to the smaller of the two flows. "There are a couple of good pools in there that usually hold fish. We'll meet you at the bottom."

Our first day on the water, and I get an entire stretch of the river all to myself?

I took off, certain that I'd have caught at least a couple by the time I saw the group again. In fact, for a while I'd been planning to catch a giant brook trout on my very first cast of the trip. Too bad everyone else would miss it.

Walking down the channel, I looked for the pools that Martin spoke of, but couldn't see any. It was boney, and there was barely a current through all the exposed rocks. Even at my young age, I could tell that this was not a great place for a trout—not even a good one.

Nevertheless, my confidence in my first-cast-fish remained. I selected the deepest and widest part, the closest thing resembling a pool; it would have to do. I made a cast and watched my size eight White Wulff—the first fly listed on the recommended list, and tied by the chef—land on the water. It drifted very slowly downstream.

A giant brook trout did not take it.

Neither did a small brook trout. Nor any fish. I made another cast, thinking that catching a fish on my second cast of the trip would be just about as good a story as catching one on my first. The same giant brook trout did not take my fly yet again. It was starting to look dire.

I fished another ten minutes or so without any luck, then decided to meet up with the others. It turned out that they'd had some success, catching a small brookie and missing another rise. At the time, I was sure that I'd been given the worse water to fish. But in reality, I was being taught the lessons of destination fishing on a steep learning curve. The reality was that the fishing was not what we thought it would be, and there was nothing that we could do about it.

We did our best to try to change the situation, though, Martin especially. As the guest, it's easy to overlook how hard a guide is working when you're focused solely on the fishing. In hindsight, I think we would've spent most of our time fishing the outlet, had the fishing been what we'd hoped. But seeing as it wasn't, over the next several days, Martin took us to spot after spot, trying to find fish for us. Just how far down his list of options we went, I'll never know.

I gained a bit of insight into this notion years later while on a guided fishing trip in New Zealand. Stu Tripney, our guide for the day, had driven us through numerous ranch gates over the course of an hour but then turned around at each road end without saying much about the reasons why. When he announced that we were going to a different river, it became clear that something was awry, so I asked him, "Is this our Plan B?"

He looked at me like I'd forgotten his name.

"'Plan B'?" he asked. "We're on Plan *Zed*, mate."

Martin took us to a couple of smaller inlets, hoping that they were running cooler and that the brookies had moved into them, but they hadn't. We also fished the lake itself, casting streamers while on anchor and then eventually trolling. The latter was a technique that I was very familiar with and was mostly disinterested in, as I'd spent many fishless hours in the front of my father's canoe back home, holding my rod at just the right angle and pulsing the fly with just the right action. So, I gave up and decided to take a nap instead. A while later, I woke up when my father missed a strike and decided that I'd try my hand at it, after all. No more than a few minutes had passed when, to Martin's delight and my father's annoyance, I caught what turned out to be the longest fish of our trip—a healthy lake trout.

Martin was excited by the capture not only because he had a happy client in his boat but also because he then had an opportunity to further apply and showcase his cooking skills. Back home, we typically regarded lake trout as by-catch and disregarded them as table fare; Martin had other plans. That night, he made a Canadian camp version of fish and chips that was so good that it's still talked about to this day. Paired with the pan-fried lake trout was the Labatt's Blue that we'd flown in. Though I was underage and hardly had a taste for it, seeing as I was the one who caught the fish, I was allowed one myself. Martin was ever-diligent and professional, though, turning down each and every offer to imbibe.

While we ate, the distinctive sound of a float plane came over camp. It was unexpected to us, but Martin didn't seem to be surprised. We all stepped outside to watch as the float plane that brought us into camp a few days prior landed again on the lake and taxied to our dock. The same pilot who delivered us stepped out.

"I heard there was a feast tonight!" he said.

It seemed Martin had radioed him to come join us. Whether to treat his friend to dinner—we had plenty of fish to share—to provide us with some entertainment, or to remove some of the conversational burden from himself was unclear. In any event, the pilot was full of yarns and jokes, and kept us laughing for the entirety of his stay. We figured that he was going to crash with us for the night, so at some point, he was offered a beer. He happily accepted and continued his fine storytelling. A while later, after drinking three or four Labatt's, he suddenly looked at his watch, jumped up, stuck his head out the camp door, and looked at the sky.

"Well, boys, that's it for me. Better get back to my camp before it gets too dark to fly, eh?" he laughed.

I was reasonably familiar with the concept (and dangers) of operating under the influence at the time, so this came as a shock to me. Looking at everyone else's faces, I could see that it was to everyone else, too; well, everyone except Martin. We quietly asked if it was alright for the pilot to take off in his current state, and Martin just shrugged. Apparently, it wasn't atypical. From the dock, we watched his plane disappear into the twilight and wondered if we'd see him again at the end of the week to fly us home.

* * *

Martin's expertise in bush cooking extended far beyond lake trout. He kept us well-fed all week, which kept spirits high despite the challenging fishing. While we initially thought that the ten-pound cast iron frying pan that he lugged around in his backpack was ridiculous, we were soon converts to it and the benefits it provided come lunchtime on the river. He cooked our lunches using the entirety of it, frying sliced potatoes in one third, cooking the small brook trout that he showed us how to target in another, and warming up biscuits or muffins in the other third. To complement lunches or when we took an afternoon break from fishing, he made bush tea by hanging a coffee pot over a fire and using ingredients he foraged from the woods.

A good, hot meal cannot be overstated in terms of its effect on clients while on a destination fishing trip. Depending on the situation, it can serve as the icing on the cake or the cake itself. Plus, it is one of a few factors that can be completely controlled by the guide or staff. In times of slow or challenging fishing, it is essentially a necessity; not catching anything is one thing, but not catching anything while being cold and hungry is simply too much to ask of a paying client. Similarly, a guide does have some flexibility in his demeanor, but only to an extent. An inspiring, cordial, conversational guide can make their way through any fishing conditions, but an asshole can only remain as such so long as everyone is catching fish. Martin turned out to be all three—a great cook, a great guy, and, as we learned by the end of the week, a great guide.

Our explorations of all the available water eventually led us to follow Martin further downstream in the lake's outlet than he had been all summer. At dinner on one of our last nights, he said that he knew of some big, deep pools in the river several miles from the lake and he suspected that the fish, which were normally spread throughout the river, were stacked up there. He hadn't fished these pools in a few seasons and couldn't remember exactly how far the hike was, but felt it was worth trying. We would need to be prepared though, and would have to carry more supplies than we had been—a full day's worth, as opposed to a half-day's. By that point, we had faith in Martin's judgment and certainly had confidence in his skills in the bush. That he was also optimistic about an out-of-the-ordinary idea encouraged and energized us as well. Over the course of the week, the challenging conditions and remote location had turned the five of us into a team. This final attempt at angling success required us all to do our part.

The next morning, we set off early, loaded down for the long day away from camp and the boats. We started by hiking to the furthest downstream pool that we'd fished before and began fishing. No fish there; we kept on. Further and further downstream we went, stopping quickly at every pool to make a few casts. Martin had brought a spinning rod with him, rigged with a hookless lure. After we made some casts with our flies, he bombed the lure across the pools. When his retrieves failed to induce any follows, we moved on. Miles passed, and still we hadn't seen the big fish that we were after. We were all a bit dejected when we stopped for lunch in the early afternoon, but again, Martin's cooking soon had us refueled and reinvigorated.

Continuing the hike downstream after lunch, it was late afternoon when we finally came to a pool bigger than any we'd seen all week. It looked like a small pond, boulder-strewn and deep and dark in the middle. We all looked at each other with nervous excitement; even Martin flashed one of his rare smiles. All that was left to do was start fishing.

Martin was right. We'd found the fish, and within an hour, we all had landed several of the brook trout that we'd dreamed of before the trip—big, strong, healthy, and vibrant beauties, residents of this lake and river system alone. The only trouble now was that we'd spent so much time getting to that big pool, and it was so far from the lake, that we had to turn back. Nevertheless, we had one more day to fish, and everyone knew exactly where we'd be spending it.

The sun had set long before we got back to the boats and crossed the lake, bound for camp in the fading light. It had been a long day, our most strenuous yet, and we were beat. Still, no one's fatigue could hide their excitement for the next day. We were tired and only going to get more tired, but we were eager for more. That we had one more day to enjoy it was almost unbelievable, for we rarely get to knowingly anticipate and experience exactly what we've dreamt about.

As often as not, a destination fishing trip doesn't yield what we come for. We start with an intended fish or quality of fishing in mind, but it isn't up to us to decide what actually happens. All we can do is to search for the fish and then see what we find. In the end, it's only what we come across along the way that we can truly take home with us anyway—memories, relationships, and stories; perhaps a keepsake. If what we came for does indeed come to pass, we do our best to recognize it, acknowledge it, and appreciate it as it happens; we taste and savor the meal that we not only ordered, but were served.

And then, when it's over, we don't forget to say thank you—mean it—and leave a good tip.

14
INTERNATIONAL PARK SKUNKING

I'm not a painter or an illustrator or a graphic artist of any sort, but I do know what I like well enough to want to capture it on paper or canvas and put it on the wall. And this was it.

Rugged peaks of impossible climbing routes towered above us in all directions. Above the tree line, snow clung to only the most shaded of crags and angles, but below it, a vibrant, glowing, and breathing forest sprawled down the hills and into the floodplain. It actually *was* breathing—the sun had just crested the torn horizon line to the east and its beams now landed on the dew-soaked limbs. They exhaled mist into the quickly warming day, where it evaporated. Below and between all these peaks and trees was a giant lake, glass-calm and mirroring the entire scene back, upside down. The surface of the lake shivered and hovered, yet retained its clarity, an enormous meniscus of reflection.

In front of us was the bay of the lake that the river ran into—the boca. The only disturbance on the lake was here, at the very beginning of the boca, where current from the river dissipated into the shallow bay before finally settling and succumbing to its seemingly stagnant existence in the lake. My eyes followed the river into the boca and then scanned down the lake and into the distance. I wondered how long it took for the water entering the lake now to make its way through to the outlet, which I couldn't see but knew existed somewhere at the other end.

To our left, the northwest, was the inlet, a river coming straight out of the Andes. That placed us in Argentine Patagonia, surrounded by a natural beauty that I didn't know existed.

"This place should be in a national park!" I said.

Nick and Paul stopped organizing their gear and glared at me.

"Is that a joke?" Nick asked.

"What? No, why? You don't think so?"

"This *is* a national park. I told you that yesterday."

I thought back. Our week had been a blur of early mornings, late nights, and unsuccessful siestas. I was exhausted. Yesterday, after a five-hour drive to reach the bottom of the lake that we now looked down on, we turned onto a slow dirt road that paralleled the southern shore, and I decided it was happy hour. One beer led to another, as they do, and apparently I'd missed or forgotten one little piece of information about the official designation of our locale.

In truth, I hadn't really known where I was since our plane left Dallas six days ago, so I didn't think it was an unreasonable question. Paul and I had flown from the States to Argentina to meet Nick. The three of us were old friends through work, but Nick, a few years younger, had left the company to do some extended traveling and fishing. I'd done the same thing years before in New Zealand and could imagine the state of mind he was in: carefree, curious, spontaneous, and on top of his angling game. When he picked us up at the airport, he was wearing sandals, revealing a bold, wading sock tan. We were in good hands.

The three of us had fished our way around the San Martin de los Andes region for most of a week, and now, as a finale to our trip, Nick had taken us to a place he considered special from both a fishing and scenery standpoint.

We continued rigging but couldn't take our eyes off the boca and the river. When a fish rose in the shallows of the lake, taking what must've been a damsel fly out of the air, it sounded like someone had thrown a baseball into the water. I nearly strained my neck turning my head so fast to catch a glimpse of the rise. We quickened our pace after that, but hurrying didn't make our preparations go any quicker. Twice my knots came undone while tightening them, and when the knot finally seated, I realized that I'd missed a guide while stringing up my rod. Nick and Paul laughed and reminded me once again that I was the last person to be ready to go fishing.

Finally, the three of us headed for the river right where it entered the lake. On our way there, we came upon what looked to be a spring creek tributary. We stopped at the first viewpoint, crouched in the grass, then looked. Three large brown trout lazily circled the pool in front of us. As if on cue, one of them ascended vertically in the water column and ate a bug off the surface in a neat rise that barely caused a disturbance on the surface.

"What do you have tied on?" Nick whispered to Paul and me.

We both held out our rods, revealing the flies we'd selected. He inspected them carefully.

"Try this," he said, handing me his rod. Put another way, I had chosen incorrectly.

I saw that he'd tied on a small, black beetle pattern, about a third of the size of my fly. I unhooked it and started to move toward the water. He grabbed my arm.

"From here," he said. "These ones are spooky."

'From here' meant that I'd be casting about sixty feet, forty-five of which was over high grass. I'd get one shot at these fish; picking up the line for a recast would be impossible.

I stripped off enough line to make the presentation, got onto my knees, and started false casting. Slowly I worked the line out of the rod tip, lengthening my casting stroke, and waiting longer and longer with each false cast, until I was ready. Then, on my final backcast before shooting line over the grass and onto the water, I fumbled the line in my hand. Losing control of the cast, sensing impending disaster but not wanting to blow the shot, I just let it go. Sixty feet of fly line landed perfectly straight in the grass directly behind us.

I looked back at the line, then at Nick and Paul. Their expressions revealed a mix of utter confusion, borderline hysterics, and I-hope-you-don't-expect-me-to-deal-with-that. I started stripping in line and the fly immediately got stuck somewhere. I turned to Nick and Paul again, this time as if a puppy who just had his toy taken away.

"I'll get it," Paul sighed.

A few minutes later, I was ready again. This time, there would be no error in the casting. I got off my knees and onto my feet, but remained hunched. As I started false casting, I slowly stood so that by the time I was ready to make my delivery, I was at about three-quarters height. I hauled and shot the line. We all watched as the cast unrolled, cleared the grass, and straightened out above the water. The line reached its limit, chirped the reel, and fell. The instant that it hit the water, the three fish scattered into the depths. The clear pool, moments ago a veritable aquarium of wild brown trout, now looked like it'd been rotenone'd. We looked at each other and shrugged.

"Let's go to the main stem," Nick said. "Those fish aren't like these ones."

We reached the river on a high, gravel bank and peered over the edge. Below us, in the middle of a deep run, finned a large brown trout in the pillow upstream of a big boulder. The fish looked happy, actively moving back and forth in the slower water. Then it rose, taking a bug off the surface quickly in a snap of its jaws. Nick was right, this was a different fish—a freestone fish, feeding like a trout ought to. Screw those paranoid and antisocial spring creek trout.

Graciously, I was again offered the shot and, figuring that I was owed some restitution for the utterly unreasonable behavior those spring creek fish had just shown me, I didn't hesitate to accept. To hell with delicacy. I fired a cast from the high bank into the middle of the river. My hopper pattern landed with a *splat*. As soon as it did, the fish went for it. I set the hook but didn't need to; the big brown was already taking line upstream. I jogged in pursuit but then stopped when I saw that the fish had done an about-face and was now headed back downstream. I reeled to keep tension, but had no leverage because of the high angle I was fighting from.

The fish knew exactly what it was doing. Helplessly, I watched as it ran around the far side of the big boulder it had been holding above and then disappeared beneath it. My rod, once bouncing, now went static, bent only by the tension of river current on lodged fly line.

The 'fish-is-gone' moment: a flood of questions and feelings followed by a simple decision to be made. Something unexpected happened; you may or may not know why, and you may or may not have liked it, but what are you going to do now? I give the fish another few seconds to reappear on the end of my line ("I'll pretend nothing happened if you do,") and when it doesn't, I break the fly off and reel in.

So, this is how it's going to be, we each thought to ourselves as we continued upstream. My opportunities to catch a fish had definitely expired for the time being, but I was happy to let someone else change our luck.

In the end, though, no one could. The fish were *there*; they fed, we hooked them, but we could not land a single one. Failed knots, tangled in a root wad, jumped and spit the hook, lost at the net, gone downstream never to return. What could've been done differently or how such a string of consecutive misfortunes could have assembled, we'll never know. Except in one instance.

The shadows were starting to get long, and it was hot. We were thirsty, hungry, and sunburned, but our feet compelled us to keep walking upstream. A fish that we could land would eventually present itself, was the logic. Reaching a braided section of the river, we split up, each of us scanning shallow channels for rising fish and those that we could spot.

In a tiny side channel of a braid, the water slowed. The flow disappeared into a cut bank on the far side, but on the inside, light sand revealed all. There, beneath the faintest of seams, was a long, dark shape on the bottom. I stopped in my tracks, took a few steps backwards, and stared at it. Tilting my head and squinting my eyes, I tried to make out a tail or fins, but couldn't. I attempted to perceive any subtle hints of motion but wasn't able. It looked just like a massive trout would have looked, except it wasn't a massive trout.

"You see one?" Nick called from downstream.

"No," I yelled to him, and then, "I don't think so..." I whispered to myself.

Inching my way forward, I unwrapped the leader from around the reel seat and reached for the fly hooked on a snake guide. The log, stick, rock, whatever, still didn't move and still didn't have fins or a tail. I took a step, unhooked the fly, and pulled some line off my reel. The whatever-it-was was still not a fish. Taking another step forward, my eyes glued to the shape, I realized that I was now no more than thirty feet away. What kind of massive trout could this be anyway, not moving with me so close?

Unless you're absolutely sure that it's not a fish, the thing to have done is casted at the log, stick, rock, whatever-it-was. And even if you are absolutely sure, you might as well cast. I say this now, because now I know.

Hooking my fly back on the snake guide, I rewrapped the leader around the reel, reeled in the slack, and walked right by the whatever-it-was. I gave it a halfway glance as I went by, and it still didn't move.

I was staring into a pool in the next braid when Nick reached the whatever-it-was.

"Are you sure that isn't a fish?" he asked, giving the shape as excruciating an inspection as I'd given it.

"Yes!" was what I said to Nick, but "It better not be" is what I said to myself, my eyes still on the pool in front of me.

Refusing to look behind me, I suddenly heard the distinctive sound of fly line being pulled slowly off a reel, and I realized that Nick was about to cast.

I spun around just in time to see Nick's fly land on the water and watch the whatever-it-was swim away.

15

THE INNER GAME OF PERMIT FISHING

The first time I went permit fishing, I caught the second fish I saw.

This statement has more than once been met with a curt, "Screw you." Call it beginner's luck, dumb luck, or whatever you want—it happened.

Prior to the trip, my only introduction to permit fishing had been a few tales from friends and Thomas McGuane's essay, "The Longest Silence." "No form of fishing offers such elaborate silences as fly fishing for permit," he wrote, before detailing several magnificent ways to lose one.

While McGuane's story did its best to curb my expectations, I'd be lying if I said I didn't think I'd get one. It could've been my ignorance or my ego talking; maybe every first-time permit angler thinks as much.

My confidence was bolstered by my boat-mates for the day. Fishing with me was Nathaniel Linville, who owns The Angling Company in Key West and is now closing in on his three hundredth permit. Guiding us was respected Keys captain Doug Kilpatrick, whose résumé includes two March Merkin and one Del Brown tournament victories.

It was February, and I had two days with this all-star duo. We launched out of Key West after several days of the coldest weather of the new year—not exactly the comfortable tropical break I'd been looking for after enduring a Pacific Northwest winter for months. The first day, with water temperatures still not quite high enough for permit, we elected to chase barracuda, also a first for me.

We left the marina early and ran to the Marquesas, twenty or so miles west of Key West. I had been there a couple of years prior to tarpon fish, but studied the islands on maps to familiarize myself with them in between my visits. To no avail, as it turned out: after we entered the interior and turned into one small bay, I was soon disoriented.

Drifting into the bay, we reviewed tactics-fly placement and retrieval, specifically. As the guest, I was offered the casting platform first, but I was happy to let Nat have the first shots. I wanted the chance to watch and get a better idea of what the game was. Listening to guides and more-experienced anglers will always be valuable, but when possible, I've found that watching them fish is just as much an education. You may not be able to replicate what they do exactly, but at least you'll know what it should look like.

In his book, *The Inner Game of Tennis*, W. Timothy Gallwey speaks to this concept of watching or "experiencing" something as a way to learn, improve upon, or emulate an action. One example he gives is of a student who has long struggled with his backhand swing but finally sees improvement after he observes his own faulty stroke in a mirror. I believe this holds true in angling, as well; especially sight fishing, where we're typically required to execute a very particular presentation to get the fish to eat. Gallwey writes, "...all good pros and students of tennis must learn that images are better than words, showing better than telling, too much instruction worse than none... [the student] simply absorbs visually the image in front of him." Through observing my companions, I soon witnessed the proper way to feed a barracuda.

With Nat on the casting platform, we spotted our first barracuda of the day. He started casting, then laid it down, his fly line landing four or five feet in front of the fish, the fly six or seven feet past it. The fish remained suspended in the water but spun ever-so-slightly towards the fly. Tucking the rod handle into his right armpit and using a two-handed strip, Nat started his retrieve slowly. As soon as he did, the fish began its move, and Nat sped up the fly. Faster and faster, he moved the fly as the fish closed the distance until demolishing it, taking it with half its mouth out of the water. The fish then took off, greyhounding away from us as the line cleared and the reel sang. In moments, it was boat-side. Looking at its teeth, I was happy to step back and let Doug show me how to safely land it.

I took the bow next, now knowing what was to be done. I made my cast; it was decent enough, so I started my retrieve, and the fish took chase. Using the same two-hand retrieve Nat had demonstrated, I stripped the fly quicker and quicker. The faster I moved the fly, the faster the fish came at it. I was moving the fly about as fast as I could when the fish finally swallowed it, and I set the hook.

As the line started to speed out of my fingers, I heard Nat call out from behind me: "Oh man, you're hosed." I looked down in time to see a softball-sized tangle of fly line bounce off the boat deck and into the stripping guide. A half-second later, the rod jolted in my hand, and the line broke.

I was to have other chances, however. The bite was on that day, to the tune of thirteen fish landed between the two of us. To put this into perspective, the winner of the prior Cuda Bowl fishing tournament (our own Nat) boated seven fish in two days to take home the title. We reasoned that the good fishing was a result of the recent colder weather; it must've been the barracudas' first day feeding on the flats since the front. As we ran back to Key West that evening, we all silently wished the same would hold for permit the next day.

The following morning, we started close to Key West and, as with the 'cuda, I was happy to let Nat have the first shots. I'd never even *seen* a permit at that point, and so decided that it might be wise to figure out what to look for, for starters. The first few fish we saw were on the move, to the point where Nat couldn't even get off much of a shot. Then, Doug called out a pair of fish approaching from behind us.

How he managed to see those fish, I'll never know. As I looked in the direction from which he said they were coming, all I saw was glare.

"Got 'em," Nat said as he began false casting. (When I say 'false casting,' I mean that he made two backcasts before sending his crab pattern eighty feet.) His cast was perfect; he stripped once, and the crab sank. A moment passed. Then another.

"He's all over it," Doug whispered.

Nat strip set the hook, and the fish took off. Line cleared, and Nat had him on the reel.

Doug came down from the poling platform, and we all exchanged high-fives. Then, as quickly as the excitement began, it ended. The fish was off, the fly had been spit. But there was no time for condolences. Doug was back on the platform, and we were again on the move, now with me on the bow.

About to take my first shot at a permit, I was armed with a fresh mental image of how it *should* go down: where the fly should land, how it should be moved, how to set the hook. The presentation Nat had just achieved wasn't complicated; it didn't involve any skill or tactic that I hadn't executed before. I just had to replicate what I'd witnessed. "...the perfect strokes are already within us waiting to be discovered," Gallwey says.

My first shot panned out like most shots at permit probably do: the fish came in quickly, I made an inaccurate cast, the fish either didn't see it or didn't like what it saw, and then it was gone. The diagnosis was easy, though—the cast simply wasn't close enough. Non-judgmental awareness is another strategy Gallwey promotes for success in *The Inner Game*. "Judgment is the act of assigning a negative or positive value to an event," he writes. "Letting go of judgments does not mean ignoring errors. It simply means seeing events as they are and not adding anything to them."

In tennis, Gallwey argues, it also takes a time or two of doing it wrong before we can do it right. I believe the same holds true for sight-fishing. "…the errors we make can be seen as an important part of the developing process," Gallwey says. With the knowledge now logged in my brain of an incorrect presentation (i.e., how far away from the fish is too far), all I had to do was adjust and take another shot.

I'd like to think that my mind was clear while we looked for another fish, my focus solely on the task at hand as opposed to reliving my failure, but this unfortunately isn't my own tendency. Forgetting past mistakes, that's another key to success in *The Inner Game*: "The greatest lapses in concentration come when we allow our minds to project what is about to happen or to dwell on what has already happened. To avoid these lapses in concentration, we must return to the here and the now… The ghosts of the past and the monsters of the future disappear when all one's conscious energy is employed in understanding the present."

I picked up a couple of shadows moving towards us just as Doug called them out as a pair of permit. When near enough, I casted.

"Good," said Doug calmly, as if responding to an inquiry over the morning's cup of coffee. The fly sank.

"Short strip." I moved the fly a half a foot.

"Let it sit." Again, the fly fell.

"Long strip."

Earlier in the day, Doug told me how he liked to call out eats to his anglers: instead of telling his clients to set the hook, he would tell them to make a *long strip*, which would actually set the hook. The idea here is that an instruction to make a supposed presentation move keeps the angler calm, as opposed to alerting them that the fish they'd traveled so far to catch has actually eaten their fly.

Sure enough, as I made my long strip, the line came into tension. Muscle memory took over, and I finished the strip firmly and sunk the hook. I carried out all these actions without wondering how to perform them or consciously thinking about any of them. This is what Gallwey refers to as *letting it happen*. "Trusting your body in tennis means letting your body hit the ball. The key word is 'let.' You trust in the competence of your body and its brain, and you let it swing the racket."

Fly line cleared without incident. The fish was on the reel, and then it took off. I nervously asked questions about rod angle and pressure, but Doug laughed them all off. "Just enjoy it," he said.

Then, the fish was in my hands.

I remember as a teen seeing pictures of permit in fly fishing magazines and telling my young fishing friends, "I want to catch a permit. They look so cool." That's certainly not the *only* reason to want to catch one, but it's a valid one. Pearlescence covered the fish. Aquamarines, matching the flat we were drifting over, reflected off its sides. Golden hues glinted off its underside. Sharp, fine black streaks covered the tops of its dorsal and tail. Our eyes, roughly the same size, met as I removed my hand from its belly and the fish re-entered the water. My other hand released its grasp over its firm and narrow tail, and the fish swam off, vanishing over the tan sandy bottom.

Does it count? Was I spoon-fed the capture? Perhaps. I did not spend years learning how to captain and pole a flats skiff. I had not spent seasons learning the flats or the tides of each. I didn't learn, through my own trial-and-error, how to present a permit fly. But I *did* see the fish, make the cast, and feed it. I hooked the fish and fought it to the boat where my guide could tail it. I did all of those things; I let them happen. I landed a permit—and I *did* enjoy it.

Many times, I've debated the advantages of employing a fishing guide versus a do-it-yourself fishing experience. While it is surely a great feeling to have "figured out" a fishery on your own, there's no question as to whether a good guide can help speed up the learning process or teach you things that you might not have learned otherwise. After studying *The Inner Game,* though, I now view the guided trip in a slightly different light: one that's much more than a lesson, an education, and the gift of a fish in the net, even though guided trips are often all of those as well.

There's an analogy Gallwey uses in his book that speaks to this. "The surfer waits for the big wave because he values the challenge it presents. He values the obstacles the wave puts between him and riding the wave to the beach. Why? Because it is those very obstacles, the size and churning power of the wave, which draw from the surfer his greatest effort. It is only against the big waves that he is required to use all his skill, all his courage and concentration to overcome; only then can he realize the true limits of his capacities…the more challenging the obstacle he faces, the greater the opportunity for the surfer to discover and extend his true potential."

I've come to believe that a great fishing guide is less a competent instructor (though they usually are that, too) and more of a companion in the angler's quest to discover and unlock their potential, helping to lead them to their 'big wave.' When the quarry is an extremely difficult fish—be it permit, tarpon, large spooky trout or otherwise—a great guide puts us in the position to unleash our best casts, to make our best presentations, and to land our most memorable fish.

If an angler were presented with an opportunity to permit fish with guaranteed success, would they accept? Probably so. But, given the chance to cast at permit all day knowing that we wouldn't land one,

I think we'd still take it. Without some failure, the value of the journey is diminished. As Gallwey writes, "The process can be more rewarding than the victory itself."

The next time I permit fish, I expect it will be hard. I won't catch them all—I may not even see one. For now, my permit count remains one.

But only until I let myself catch another one.

16
ONE BEER

New Zealand's hut system is an extensive network of public trails and cabins of varying sizes and conditions, providing lodging to anyone willing to make the trek. For those fond of old cottages, lodges, or fishing camps, they are sure to please. Some are better-kept than others, and some house more rodents than humans, but all of them are worth a visit, if not to admire their distinctive designs and characteristics, then certainly to enjoy their surroundings. Many of the huts sit on worthwhile trout rivers as well, offering a temporary home base from which to fish multiple days or access water too remote for day trips.

When someone first described the hut system to me, I couldn't imagine why anyone interested in backpacking would stay anywhere else. The system only got better when I learned that there was an annual pass—for the unbelievable price of $60, I could have unlimited stays at as many huts as I could hike to! As soon as I learned about the pass, I started planning fishing around the locations of huts.

The official hut system is managed by the country's Department of Conservation, and there are nearly a thousand of them peppered across the North and South Islands. They vary in size from two bunks ('bunks' meaning beds, not bunk beds) to over twenty. Most are equipped with the same standard furnishings: mattresses, wood stove, dining table and seating, candle or lantern lighting, outhouse, and a water source. The latter is sometimes piped inside the hut but can also be in the form of a water pump or even a nearby river or stream. That the huts take the place of a tent, sleeping pad, and water for the entirety of a trip makes them ideal stops on backpacking trips.

The first hut that I had the pleasure of staying in was the Hope Halfway Hut, located a half-day's hike up the Hope River. My first night there also featured my first campfire in New Zealand, something I'd been looking forward to since I arrived a couple of weeks prior. I burned the embers down to nothing that night, alternating my gaze between their orange glow and the silver spots in the sky above me. The next day, I cast to so many giant, dry fly-eating browns that I was miles away from the hut by the time it turned to twilight; I just couldn't stop. When I finally got back to the hut, I consumed three packages of a ramen noodle knock-off and immediately passed out.

Then there was the Manson-Nichols hut, where I met two brothers on their annual backpacking trip. When they arrived, I'd already eaten my noodle dinner, and I was reading a book in my bunk. I watched with one eye as they unloaded bottles of wine, cheeses, meats, and breads from their packs. They made a massive, decadent spread and then demanded that I join them. I half-heartedly objected, saying that I had already eaten and that they weren't obligated to share. "I saw the package of what you ate," one of the brothers said, pointing to the trash can. "That's not dinner, mate."

Lakehead Hut was the busiest of the ones I visited. My first night there, I (and the rest of the hut's occupants) listened to an excruciatingly annoying doctor from the States ramble on about various and obscure health-related topics and his wisdom thereon. He was on a honeymoon trip and I presume trying to exhibit his worldliness to his new bride (not an unrelatable nor unadmirable task, though I question the tactic). After he finished denouncing tobacco and all of its users, I retrieved my pouch, rolled a cigarette at the table, and excused myself from the conversation for good. When everyone in the hut was falling asleep, I heard him whispering to his partner, "I didn't brush my teeth, dear, but I flossed, which is much more important to gum health anyway."

Thankfully, the doctor and his partner departed the next day and were replaced by a young Kiwi family. I spent that evening around a campfire with the parents and their two young girls, eating s'mores and sharing stories. The girls were much better conversationalists than the doctor. When I left the following morning to go fishing, I found that the girls had pranked me by hiding marshmallows in my wading boots. I happily consumed the sugar bombs on my way to the river, chuckling as I imagined the girls performing the stunt.

At Upper Oreti Hut, on the tail end of a week-long stint in the bush, with food supplies very low, four of us spent the evening sharing daydreams of elaborate meals we wished to consume, if only someone would deliver them by helicopter: bacon cheeseburgers, supreme pizzas, wet burritos, ribs, and chicken wings. We knew it was self-torture, but we also knew that we would be heading back to civilization (and a pub) the next day.

The list goes on. Alone on New Year's Eve, I secreted a bag of red wine into Captain's Hut and, under its influence, wrote an epic resolutions list that went on for several pages. Mansion Hut was by far the smallest we stayed in, with barely enough room for two bunks, a small table, and a fireplace. Conversely, Cannibal Gorge Hut was an eighteen-bunk palace, and we had that one all to ourselves as well. The fishing while at Blowfly Hut was very good and seemed to be inspired by the hut's name—we didn't tie on a single nymph for three days.

A number of the rivers I fished and huts that I stayed in were suggestions from my new friend and longtime New Zealand fishing guide, Chappie Chapman. Chappie and I fished for several days shortly after I arrived, and he gave me a proper introduction to the country and its trout fishing. He was generous in sharing his knowledge of fishing and geography, going so far as to review pages and pages of maps with me. It didn't take me long to realize that every circle he made was worth visiting. Located roughly halfway up the west coast of the South Island, one particular hut was at the confluence of a main stem and a tributary, offering two solid days of water to explore in both directions. Chappie winked as he marked it.

The plan was straightforward. I'd leave my van in the gravel pit at the road's end, hike to the hut along the dirt track that followed the river, and start fishing from there. Though it was summer and daytime temps were high, the dense forest kept the undergrowth cool and damp. It had also rained recently, and at my feet, the trail consisted of wide, deep mud-holes that started out bad and got worse as I went. At first, I laughed at the state of the track, but my good humor was lost when I slipped and crashed in the middle of one. After falling for a second time, I was soaked, covered in mud, and livid. I yelled into the forest, demanding respite. I cursed the track, my mud-filled boots, and the hut that wouldn't appear. Wet and muddy, the six miles felt more like sixteen.

After the slog, the hut finally came into view. It sat in a small clearing overlooking the river. The door hinges creaked open, and I scanned the room skeptically before stepping inside. It had clearly been a while since anyone had visited. The air was dank, the bunks were dust-covered, and cobwebs curtained the windows and filled the woodstove. It was the only hut I'd visited that made me wish I'd brought a tent to sleep in instead. A few well-used utensils sat on a shelf next to a single can of Speights beer, "Pride of the South." I studied it and considered sampling, but guessed it to be lukewarm and likely skunked.

I decided to check out the river instead. As soon as I did, thoughts of the grueling trail instantly dissolved. From outside the hut, I looked down at the tailout of a quintessential South Island trout run and saw a large brown trout happily rising to mayflies. The paper-white inside of its mouth sharply contrasted with its golden body. I watched as long as I could take it, and then got my gear ready.

One cast was all it took. He tipped my net-scale at just over seven pounds. Euphoria set in. All was right and everything made sense now: the dreadful hike was just the cost of admission. The stellar fishing was the reward for my efforts. And I was just getting started.

It would've taken a disaster to kill my high as I fished out the day. The weather was perfect and the trout were on the feed. When the sun dropped, I turned back and walked the riverbed toward that first fateful pool and the hut that sat on the small bluff above it. I'd been hiking downstream for some time, lost in the memories of the day, when I looked up and realized that I was totally lost.

With daylight waning, I assessed the situation, then poked my head into the forest and spotted something familiar: the hellacious dirt track full of knee-deep mud puddles. I laughed again at its ridiculous condition as well as the conflicting doses of karma it represented. While I'd been compensated with some nice trout for my earlier efforts on the hike in, I was now paying the price for complaining about it. The track that I'd cursed earlier was now my only way back, and there was no escaping its muddy embrace.

A certain thirst came over me as I neared the hut that evening. I opened the door, dropped my gear, and went straight for the can of Speights. To my pleasant surprise, it was cold to the touch. I cracked it open, smelled it, and took a hesitant sip. It couldn't have tasted better.

I toasted the river, the hut, then New Zealand, and chugged the rest.

17
EFFORTLESS & PRETTY

Years ago, after an encounter-less day on the Salmon River in upstate New York, a friend of mine affectionately referred to as Dr. Steelegood and I decided that swinging flies for steelhead is like being up to bat, only you're blindfolded, and also the pitcher doesn't actually throw the ball every pitch.

That's the glass-half-empty take on the whole endeavor, and exceptions certainly exist, but consider this: both the batter and steelheader take swings in attempts to achieve their ultimate goals; a fundamentally sound cut with the bat and the picture-perfect cast may be, and statistically speaking usually are, unrewarded; and the batter and the angler are all alone in their areas of work—the batter's box and the river.

Of course, we can debate what the ultimate goal is. I'm pretty sure any big-league hitter loves watching a ball fly over the fence, but I bet they also love the sound of the crowd as they near the box, the feel of the dirt under their spikes, the intensity of staring into a pitcher's eyes. Thankfully, my own paycheck doesn't depend on the number of steelhead I tail each season.

I often over-analyze the situation when I'm "in the box." Do I have the right fly on? Do I need a heavier sink-tip? Should I mend more? Less? Is this even good water? Are there steelhead in this river? Should I have eaten pancakes instead of a breakfast burrito? What exactly are we doing out here? Confidence undeniably hooks more fish, so a restless mind must be quieted.

The simple answer is that we're trying to catch a fish. The less simple answer is that we're trying to catch a particular fish in a certain way; we are trying to put the right fly in front of the right fish with the right presentation. Of those three criteria, I've come to believe that the first doesn't matter much, the second you can't control, and the third is very difficult.

With so much time between encounters, steelheading provides little feedback. To get the right presentation, there are many variables an angler can experiment with, should they choose to: fly size, fly dress, fly weight, leader length, leader diameter, sink-tip density, sink-tip length, casting direction, amount of mend, steps after cast, how you steer it… those are just a few I can think of. And they all change when you change water.

I've been fortunate to make friends with an outfit of veteran steelhead guides in the Pacific Northwest. Their techniques are varied, covering fly sizes ten to four-inch articulateds at depths of zero to ten feet. Having dinner together prior to a trip, we asked our guide Whitney what length leaders they had been fishing.

"Precisely three to thirteen feet," she said with a smirk.

On another trip, I talked myself and our guide Mike into a maze of presentation tactics. (Or perhaps I should say, I asked my way there.) '*Why are we using a certain sink-tip, fly, and leader here?*' "To achieve presentation X," he answered. '*How do you know this rig will do that?*

And why do we want the fly to do that here?' I felt like a child with question after question, why after why's. In this case, the why's are probably a function of experience that I simply don't (and likely won't ever) possess.

Mike did his best to answer my questions, and eventually, I was satisfied enough to start fishing. As I stepped into the head of the run and started peeling off line, he came beside me and gave the best pure fishing advice I've ever received.

He said:

"The cast must go the necessary distance,

In the appropriate direction.

At the end of the cast, the lure should turn over (most of the time).

It should be effortless and pretty."

I made Mike write it down that night in camp so I wouldn't forget. In an arena where you can control only a third of the game, it's good to hang onto whatever tips you can get. Sometimes, answers to the simple questions can help quiet the bigger ones.

The next day, I got into the same conversation with one of the other guides. His patience for my unrelenting questions wasn't as long as Mike's, and after three or four queries about how various sink-tip and leader lengths affected presentation, he just said, "Dude, it doesn't matter! Get in the water!" I got the message, stepped into the run, and promptly stuck a fish. Sometimes it truly doesn't make a difference, so long as your fly's actually in the water.

The first time I fished in British Columbia, three friends and I were helicoptered into as magnificent a steelhead water as one could think of—the Dean River. I reached the river with at least a hundred flies. While this tally eased my mind in preparing for the trip, it would turn out to be a hindrance when I was riverside, about to make my pass through a greasy run. Every time I reached a new piece of water or changed flies, I found myself hunched over the fly box, three or four patterns in each hand, contemplating and debating the merits of each.

I was determined to catch my first fish on a fly I had tied, and succeeded in this on the second day. The pattern that took off my skunk was a three-inch, unweighted red, orange, and pink Popsicle-style shank-fly. I then switched over to a fly tied by my roommate at the time, James. His fly hooked fish on back-to-back casts! The first was a fresh hen of about eight pounds that I tailed a few hundred yards downstream, and the next was a ten-inch smolt.

Several days later, I found myself in a bit of a slump. I was reaching the end of my second consecutive fishless day and was becoming frustrated with my casting, hanging up on bottom, putting D-loops into bushes, and feeling generally un-fishy. I ended the day by losing three flies in the same run. I told myself that the fish didn't want to eat those flies (another handy excuse), and took to the bank to collect myself and take in the scene while my friend finished the run. I made these realizations: the three flies I just lost were store-bought, and all the flies I'd taken fish on were either tied by me or someone I knew. I concluded then that flies without soul, or that I didn't have a personal connection to, would not work. More veteran steelheaders have enjoyed this realization for decades, but for me, it happened when it happened. I spent the rest of the trip fishing flies that fit this description.

With this new knowledge, my fly box was halved. Choosing which fly to tie on was still difficult, though. I think nearly all the patterns in my box would've worked, but for any number of reasons, only a few felt good to me at times. I guess it didn't matter if it took me ten seconds or ten minutes to pick my fly, so long as the one I did choose felt right.

Two years later, I returned to the Dean, this time with a pile of exclusively soulful flies. Before the trip, I also read an essay by the Northeast angler, tyer, and artist Ken Abrames, in which he spoke of changing flies after each striped bass he caught as a way to learn about the patterns, colors, and sizes that would take fish. I decided that I was going to adopt this approach on the Dean, to try to get confirmation on some of my own ties, and also because it sounded like fun. By that time, I was getting pretty keen on the notion that fly pattern didn't make a huge difference, at least to the fish, so what better place to fish a bunch of untested patterns?

Thus, as the shadows got long that first day, right after I landed my first steelhead of the trip, I went for it. It seemed insane to cut off the fly that I had just caught a fish on. But sure enough, shortly after changing flies, I caught another fish. I ended up landing ten that trip, all on different patterns.

The following winter, I was at bat on a coastal Washington state river. The pitcher was really throwing heat. I got yanked in a tailout but lost the fish when I attempted to fight it with my rod tip in a tree. I reeled in and walked upstream to meet my buddy, who was taking his turn.

"Nice work," he said. "Tough spot to fight one."

I shrugged.

"And did I see you changing flies in the middle of that pass?"

I laughed and showed him the fly.

"What do you think?" I asked. "Was it the fly, the fish, or the presentation?"

He raised an eyebrow while spinning the fly in his fingers.

"Yes."

PART III
EVERYWHERE

WHEREVER IT IS, FLY FISHING IS DISTINCTLY THE SAME

18
TOO MANY

I check the clock, do the math, and dial. He answers on the first ring, puts me on speakerphone.

"Old Man."

He calls me Old Man because I was the first of our friends to get gray hair.

"Pete. What are you doing?"

"Rolling cigarettes. Going fishing. Can't talk long."

Living on the opposite coast from fishing friends makes it hard to stay in touch. A three-hour time difference doesn't seem like much, but sometimes it's just enough.

Pete's fishing program is unlike most of my angling friends'. He's a shore-based, wetsuit-wearing, Cape Cod striped bass fisherman, and he selectively fishes certain tides, exclusively under the cover of night. As mentioned before, I'm more accustomed to the early-to-bed, early-to-rise type of fishing, so the few times I joined him threw off my biological clock for a couple of days afterward. (Did I just admit to being an old man?)

Despite our time differences—geographically and fundamentally—we're still old fishing buddies, so we talk when we can and pick up where we left off. My well-timed call from the West Coast finds him on the East Coast in pre-fishing preparations, which is always a fun time to chat.

"I thought you might be," I say. "How many do you need?"

"'*How many do I need?*'"

"Yeah, how many cigarettes do you need to go fishing?"

"Oh…too many."

I consider this in silence for a moment. Pete and I often get into philosophical debates over angling minutia, and I have to choose my next words carefully. I'm usually good for a few rounds of back-and-forth, but here was a proposition I immediately struggled with.

Sensing my lack of understanding, he adds: "I don't know how long I'll fish, and I don't want to waste time rolling them when I'm out there, so it's best to have too many."

I admit defeat before even attempting a rebuttal.

"Makes sense to me. How's the fishing?"

He laughs, knowing he won the debate.

"I'm about to find out. I'll call you tomorrow and let you know. See ya, Old Man."

He hangs up, and I think about what he said. "Too many" is not a number that jibes with my own analytical disposition, but after some thought, I realize that I employ a similar approach with an angling accessory of my own: flies. I think about my numerous boxes with rows upon rows full of flies. I quickly dismiss the notion that there's a countless quantity and calculate an estimate of how many I have, starting with my trout flies. Using round numbers for easy math gives me a fly box with two sides of ten rows at twenty flies per row; looking into my hip pack, I count four boxes. So, that's sixteen hundred flies, and that's just what I carry. That doesn't include the half-dozen other fly boxes in my trout fishing boat bag, or the other boat bags. It's staggering and frankly embarrassing.

The reasonings behind Pete's reserve of cigarettes and my stockpiles of flies are analogous but nuanced. While his philosophy requires an unspecified but very large supply of a singular ingredient, mine relies on precise quantities of a high number of specific variations. Neither approach is better than the other, yet both are equally as important to the mission. In either case, the worst possible scenario is to run out.

Despite my seemingly endless inventory, I can easily recall a time when I did *not* have enough flies. I was driving from Wyoming to Washington and pit-stopped to fish a small trout stream in Idaho. It was late summer, and even though I was on the water early, it was already bright and getting hot. Seeing a few caddis and a mayfly or two, I started by trying several relevant imitations.

No luck. I then decided to tie on my favorite hopper pattern—a tan Schroeder's Parachute. At the next piece of good-looking water, I saw a refusal and realized there was a player. I downsized my fly and tied on a cinnamon-colored Turck's Power Ant. The fish took it on the next cast.

Continuing upstream, I quickly caught a couple more, then noticed that the fly was starting to unravel. I checked my boxes for another but couldn't find one. I decided to try another ant pattern, about the same size, but black and without the rubber legs. I tied it on and resumed fishing. Nothing happened.

Finally, after fishing it in a pool that looked too good, I tied the chewed-up Power Ant back on, and immediately rose a fish. I kept fishing the fly—and catching fish—until there was only a fragment left; it wasn't floating, didn't look like an ant, and the fish finally weren't interested anymore.

But I knew they were still feeding.

I tried another ant pattern, then a beetle, and then the smallest hopper I could find. None worked. I went back to what I started with—caddis, mayflies…same as before. Convinced that anything else wouldn't work, I took one last, half-hearted look for another cinnamon Power Ant. Unsuccessful, I called it a day.

No amount of preparation is enough to satisfy every possibility. We try our best, compiling thousands of flies and rolling dozens of cigarettes, attempting to control the outcome in our favor. Eventually, we run out of whatever it may be. These moments leave us frustrated and temporarily unfulfilled, but ultimately we benefit, for that which we desire is fleeting and finite. Little excitement would be had if we always knew the right fly and had plenty of it; the cigarette would not satisfy nearly so well if it never went out, nor would we crave to light another. Wish as we may for never-ending time on the water, our angling days are numbered, and that is why we value them so dearly.

I asked Pete recently if he had ever run out of cigarettes while fishing.

"I never ran out," he said. "But one time I left them behind."

It was after midnight, and he had kayaked a couple of miles through the remnants of a tropical storm to an island from which he could access a deep channel with heavy current. After realizing that he left his tobacco behind, he immediately turned around, kayaked back to his truck, grabbed the pouch, and paddled back to the island again.

"I immediately rolled what was sure to be the best cigarette ever," he told me.

"But after all that, I forgot the damn lighter."

19
EVERYTHING THAT HAPPENS

We bounce up the narrow dirt road in Scott's old Ford Bronco toward the boat launch. The rear bench seat upon which I sit is very squishy—not unlike the truck's suspension—and is covered in worn, blue leather. It's comfortable but is permanently reclined at an angle that feels a bit too relaxed. I could see watching a movie in such a position, but I'm too excited to lean back. Steelheading is more of an on-the-edge-of-your-seat event, especially at six-something in the morning after two cups of coffee.

Driving over a couple of potholes, the door starts rattling, and the dome light blinks. Without missing a beat or slowing down, Scott opens the door and slams it shut so hard that it makes me flinch. The rattling stops. It feels like I'm on some odd safari ride with an eccentric matched pair of vehicle and guide.

At the sharp bends, the lanes narrow further still. The cliff walls close in on us, and the margin of error between driving on the road and tumbling into the river below shrinks. Going around one such bend, a handful of bowling ball-sized rocks appear in the middle of the road. Scott swerves to dodge them, but there isn't much room to work with. We hit one straight on, and everyone inside the truck bounces a few inches out of their seats. The truck takes the rock well enough, but the trailer behind us doesn't, and we all hear it crash over the rock. The raft that it carries bucks but thankfully stays strapped down.

"There it goes again," Scott grumbles. "Can you stop and grab that on your way back?"

I turn around in my seat just in time to see a trailer light fixture lying in the road disappear around the corner. Beyond the edge of the road is the river, and I can see a beautiful steelhead run just becoming visible in the gray light.

"Jesse?"

He's talking to me.

"Huh?"

"You're driving this back to the lodge, right?" Scott asks.

"Oh yeah, right."

"Grab that trailer light on your way back, please."

"Yeah, sure thing," I say, my eyes still on the river behind us.

I look around the Bronco. Of the four people inside, I'm the only one not dressed in waders, a reminder that I'm not going fishing. Not yet anyway. This morning, I'm the shuttle driver. It's the least I can do, seeing as Scott is letting me camp on his property *and* is feeding me for the week.

In a few more minutes, we arrive at the put-in. Scott backs the trailer down, hops out of the truck, and begins sliding the raft off.

The rest of us busy ourselves and collect the rods from the roof racks. One in particular catches my eye: a brand-new fiberglass Spey rod. I ask about it, seeing as I've never cast one. The owner, one of Scott's two clients for the day, offers to let me try it before they push off.

So, as Scott and the two anglers organize their gear, I walk up the gravel bar a ways to make a few Single Spey casts, and get a feel for the rod.

Suddenly, headlights flash from upstream. We all turn and look as a pickup with distinctive colors pulls onto the gravel bar: Fish and Wildlife. A man dressed in a navy blue uniform steps out of the truck and makes his way toward Scott and the anglers. I can't make out their conversation exactly, but judging from the reactions of the anglers, the officer is checking their fishing licenses. I take another couple of casts, reel in, and start walking back to the group.

By the time I get there, Scott has unpacked two dry boxes from his raft and is shuffling through several plastic bags filled with papers while the officer watches. He needs to show the man a variety of articles: his guide's license, a Bureau of Land Management permit, life jackets, wag bags, whistle, all of it. The whole process takes nearly ten minutes.

After satisfying the legal matters, Scott repacks the boat. The officer then turns to me.

"Can I see your fishing license, please?"

"Oh, I'm not fishing right now. I'm just driving the shuttle."

"What about that rod you're holding? I just saw you casting it," he says, straight-faced. "I see there's a fly tied on."

I quickly realize that he's serious. What's worse, he's technically right—I have indeed been fishing. But it's also obvious that I'm not joining Scott and the other anglers: I'm dressed in Carhartts and rubber boots. I explain the situation and note that while I do have a fishing license, it's in my waders, back at Scott's lodge.

It seems to work. "OK," says the officer, "so you're driving the shuttle. Then let me see your driver's license."

I pat my back pocket where my wallet usually resides. There's nothing in it.

"Right. So, my driver's license is *also* back at the lodge," I explain.

Scott and his clients are grinning at me when, all of a sudden, the distinctive sound of a truck and trailer bouncing on a dirt road comes over the boat launch. Someone else is about to put in.

"Dammit," Scott mutters. "OK, guys, let's go!"

For Scott, a career steelhead guide and lodge owner, another boat on the water complicates things in a few ways. Another group of anglers—or possibly another guide with clients—could beat him to certain spots on the river that he wants to fish with his own clients. But another consideration is that the other group could potentially see where—and further, *how*—Scott is fishing. Obvious runs are one thing, but Scott has a number of less-than- and much-less-than-obvious spots where he knows how to hook steelhead. He does not want anyone else to see and steal his hard-won intel, especially when the success of his clients is at risk.

Whether aware of it or not, anyone Spey casting for steelhead in the Pacific Northwest has been influenced in some way by Scott. He pioneered casting and fishing techniques that are now standardized; he's often referred to as a "casting instructor's instructor." For those who are passionate about this type of fishing in this place, he is as much of a celebrity as there is—a living legend. He's also one of the most sought-after guides in the region, not only for his dedication, expertise, and instructional abilities but also for his company; his kind-heartedness, sarcastic sense of humor, and storytelling chops make him a delight to fish with.

I know Scott well enough by now to know all this. But like the masters of any field, his passion is so deep that it sometimes affects his demeanor. I know when he's upset and when it's time to leave him be. This is one of those times.

Scott drags the raft into the river, and the anglers hop in. I've fished with Scott on this beat several times before and know that he typically fishes the run at the put-in, so the fact that he's now skipping it tells me that he's already strategizing, coming up with workarounds for this second boat that's about to launch. He tosses the anchor in the boat and starts pushing downstream just as the other truck and trailer pulls onto the gravel bar.

"I'll see you back at the lodge tonight," he calls to me as the raft floats away. "Don't fish anything ahead of us!"

I wouldn't dare.

The officer and I watch them disappear downstream. Judging by the pace he's rowing and his posture, I can tell Scott isn't pleased and that his day's fishing program has already been compromised by this other boat. I try to imagine what's going through his mind, a chess game of possibilities, each weighing both offense—arriving at good water first and stopping to fish it—and defense—getting far enough downstream so that the other boat will have to stop first themselves.

I'm still trying to guess where Scott's headed when the officer breaks my trance. "Bring your driver's license the next time you're driving the shuttle," he instructs. "Have a good day."

I thank him, say that I will, and climb into the Bronco. I gently ease it off the gravel bar and onto the dirt road, then head back for the lodge. I grab the trailer light, still waiting patiently for me in the middle of the road, and plan out the rest of my day.

My aim is to gear up, drive upstream again in my own truck, and then fish my way back toward the lodge, working behind Scott and his anglers. I'll be fishing some water they'll have already gone through, but that's still a pretty good deal for free camping and meals. I putter around camp a bit, eat a late breakfast, and slowly get my things together. I want to give them some time to get downstream and leave me with a few choices of water.

By the time I'm ready, a couple of hours have passed. I double-check that I have all my licenses and start upriver. The sky is lighter now, and

I can easily see the river from the road. Driving slowly, I peer out the window and gauge the quality of each run that I pass.

I barely make it a mile up the road when I see three figures standing in the river. I stop the truck and stare, trying to make out who they are. I look at the clock; it's just after 10:30 am. I didn't see any other boats on the water on my way back to the lodge earlier. It can't be Scott or the other boat—it's much too early for either of them to be this far downstream in the float.

I inch forward in the truck, then stop again.

Sure enough, it's Scott and his guys. And something is definitely off. Scott knows this river, and this float specifically, better than almost anyone. If you told him that you caught a steelhead in a certain run, he could tell you what tree was across the river from where you hooked it. If you told him you fished a certain run and *didn't* hook a fish, he'd tell you what you did wrong, which could include you fishing there in the first place. One time he came up to me in the middle of a run and said, "You're fishing this like someone who doesn't want to catch a steelhead." He knows what he's doing, so it's tough for me to believe that he's mismanaging his time on the water. Yet based on the clock and where he is, there's only one more run to fish in and about six hours to do it.

As I near them from the road, I roll down the window and stick out my hand. I can't tell if Scott sees me or not, but either way, he doesn't wave back. I don't press the issue and continue upstream.

I fish the day away and head back to the lodge at dusk. Walking to dinner, I bump into one of Scott's clients from the day; I'm guessing it didn't go so well. I also know that I shouldn't let on that I saw them way out of place in the beat early in the morning.

"Hey, how was your day?" I ask, as cheerfully as I can.

"That Scott is something else," he says, visibly intoxicated. "We got two awesome fish, and one on a dry fly! What a way to end the week."

We walk together, and he tells me about the fight and how big the fish was. When we reach the lodge, Scott is standing under the porch light, smoking a cigarette in the mist. The client goes inside, leaving Scott and me.

"What happened out there?" I whisper so no one inside can hear. "I saw you way downstream at like ten o'clock...but you got two fish?"

He lets out a laugh. "That damn boat..." he says, shaking his head. "I stopped at the next run downstream from the put-in, thinking that they'd fish the run at the launch. But they didn't—they passed me before we fished even half of the run that we were in."

I could see where this was going.

"So we took off downstream," he continues, "and I'm thinking that we'll leapfrog them right back. But they must've been rowing hard because I couldn't catch up. I kept thinking that I'd see them pulled over, but they didn't stop! I rowed by six spots that I usually fish until I finally saw them. They were fishing in some weird spot, one I've never caught a fish in. I pushed past them and went another couple of runs just to make sure that we wouldn't see them again..."

The lodge door bursts open, and one of Scott's clients sticks his head out. There's a tall glass of whiskey in his hand.

"Scott—tell these guys how big that fish was! They don't believe me!"

Scott smiles. "I told you, it was all of eight pounds!" The room erupts.

"What?! Liar!" the client says. "That's not what you told me! You said it was thirteen!"

He slams the door, and it's quiet again outside.

"By then," Scott resumes, "I realized how far I'd floated and that I was kind of screwed. There were only three more big runs in the float, and it wasn't even ten o'clock yet. Of the three runs left, the middle one is the best, and I couldn't risk having that other boat get there before me. So I pushed right through the first one to get there. Now I had two runs left: a great one and one that's so-so. I saw you drive by and wave, but I was too pissed to say hi. Sorry about that."

"All good. So what happened?"

"Well, we fished that run hard. I had each of them take two passes with different rigs each time and had them one-step it. I was sure we'd get one, but we didn't. By now it's almost one o'clock, so I push down to the next run, the last one on the float. And it's not really looking that good.

"I get the chairs and table out, and we have lunch. That takes an hour or so, but while we're eating, the sun comes out and now I have to kill some more time. So, I get the stove out and make some coffee. Thankfully, the clouds come back while we're doing that. I re-rig their setups completely and put a skater on one. I was figuring that we'd have to make two or three passes each to finish out the day, so we might as well work our way down the water column.

"The first guy steps into the run and on his fourth cast, a fish explodes on the dry fly and goes bananas. I don't know how that fish stayed hooked, but somehow it did, and we landed it; a gorgeous wild hen. The guys are stoked, and I'm feeling pretty relieved.

"I pulled out the old bottle of schnapps that I keep in the dry box, because why the hell not, and now it seems like killing time might not be such a bad thing. We're standing there on the gravel bar drinking schnapps, celebrating that fish, and that damn boat floats by! I never figured out what they were doing, but I'm pretty sure I messed up their program, so *that* felt good."

I chuckle and shake my head, imagining just what the guys in that other boat could have been thinking as they floated by Scott and his clients, mid-afternoon, drinking a bottle of schnapps on a gravel bar, two hundred yards from his lodge.

"So finally, I send the second guy into the run…and he gets one, too!"

Scott takes a long drag off his cigarette and exhales. The smoke dissolves into the evening air. An owl hoots in the distance and we hear another round of laughter from inside the lodge.

"I couldn't believe it," he says quietly.

"But," he pauses, staring into the darkness, "I guess everything that happens is just leading you to your next steelhead."

I raise my eyebrows and look at him, taking in the depth of the statement and the weight of it all. The man before me has dedicated his life to steelhead fishing and sharing it with others. After four decades of fishing and guiding, it's still his "everything," and he still does whatever he can to make sure that his clients have great days on the water.

The moment lingers. I don't have anything to add.

"What about you?" he asks. "Find any?"

"Me? Oh, no, not today," I say.

"No?" he smiles and opens the lodge door. "Well, where were you fishing?!"

20
ON STEALTH

Sheridan Anderson's primer *The Curtis Creek Manifesto* is a lovely introduction to fly fishing. In it, he wastes no time informing aspiring anglers that stealth is of utmost importance: "Thou shalt move with stealth and keep thyself low and in deepest shadow and ever secret thyself behind tree, rock, hummock, and shrub." He discusses the merits of upstream presentations for secrecy's sake and dedicates a spread in the book to the art of stalking, including "The Upstream Crawl." It's obvious to any reader that secrecy is essential and, should they wish to fool a fish into taking their fly, they need not be heard nor seen.

As a young'un, I'd take an annual trip with my father, 'Uncle' John, and Wilkie to a remote pond in northern Maine to fish ice-out. The pond is notoriously slow, but big, native brookies live there, and we considered landing one in a day a success. One year, halfway through a rather sluggish session, Wilkie and I decided against cruising the shoreline in our square stern canoe to instead post up on a large rock pile and fish from there, on foot. It's a fishy spot, offering great structure and access to deeper water. Over the years, we fished from or around the rock pile often, and the spot had produced for us perhaps as well as any other on the pond.

We were nearing the rock pile, the small outboard humming, when I felt our course change. I assumed that Wilkie wanted to approach the rock pile from a different angle, but when our direction didn't change and the wide turn started to turn into a big circle, I looked back at him. Wilkie had given up his grip on the tiller and was hunched over, attending to something I couldn't see. Annoyed, I fired some criticism.

"Oh, come on," he spat back. "It doesn't make a difference."

Wilkie is older, more experienced, and it was his boat, so I held my tongue. But I felt certain that our entrance had screwed us. Eventually, we made it to the rock pile and started fishing. We casted in silence for the next hour, each of us stewing until the skunk set in and we moved to another spot.

Years later, when I arrived in New Zealand, I had a few days booked with Chappie Chapman, the veteran South Island guide. While rigging up for the day, he noted my brand new fly line, the head of which was colored lime green. The bright color was of no use to us that day, he informed me, for we'd surely spook our targets. After our day's fishing, he suggested that I color my fly line with a dark-green permanent marker, or simply buy a new one. I took the message seriously and was at a local fly shop the next day to acquire a "Camo Green" colored line.

A few months after fishing with Chappie, I had a trip with another guide, Stu Tripney, who lived further south. Stu's stance on fly line color was starkly opposite, for his reels were all spooled with various color lines, including fluorescent green, orange, and even bright pink. I quizzed him on this, and he seemed delighted to inform me that the color of my fly line did not matter. To prove his point, he showed me a video in which he caught a large brown trout on a white fly rod and pink fly line…while casting through the sunroof of his Land Cruiser. I didn't dare try to fool a New Zealand trout on my own with a bright pink fly line, but I have done it in the States since.

Another time, while steelheading in Oregon, my friends Paul and Andy and I made an early departure from camp to arrive at a specific piece of water as close to first light as we could. Andy, who knew the river well, had come up with the plan. The fact that it was a different approach than we had been taking in the days prior led me to believe that our timing was critical. We floated past several good-looking runs in the early morning light, and when the spot in question appeared downstream, the strategy was discussed in hushed tones.

"Paul, I'm going to drop you off in the middle of the river on that gravel bar," Andy said. "Jesse and I will anchor up on the far shore while you fish it. Get one."

With short, soft oar strokes, we slowed down at the gravel bar and Paul quietly slid out of the raft. We left him there and with hardly a sound made our way to the opposite side of the river. Paul gently stripped line off his reel, preparing to make his first cast. Meanwhile, our raft was nearing the bank. Andy carefully set the oars in the water, grabbed his anchor, and tossed it.

KABOOM!

I whirled around in my seat, surprised and thinking some mistake had been made. But Andy's body language didn't indicate as such. I could just barely see Paul in the middle of the river, staring at us with raised hands in irritated confusion. Realizing that no explanation would be given, he started fishing. No steelhead were encountered, and the incident was not discussed until Paul and I were alone later that evening. Neither of us could come up with any reasonable explanation.

Later that same trip, on a day when no one had touched a fish, we were reeling in at the end of a run when a couple of boats appeared upstream.

"Hold on," Andy said. "Let these boats float through, then take another pass."

I was skeptical, and I could tell Paul was too. But he obliged the request and went to the top of the run. Sure enough, halfway through the piece, he got one. After he released it, Paul and I caught eyes and just shrugged. I've heard of other such occurrences since; some steelheaders swear by it. Why then do we all pull into steelhead runs as close to the head as possible?

A few summers after that trip, I visited my friend Drew who guided for smallmouth in northeast Wisconsin at the time. I planned my visit to coincide with what he said was the best topwater bite of the season, and it appeared I'd hit it right. For three days, we found willing fish wherever they should've been and even where they probably shouldn't have. However, our last day on the water was just the opposite—we couldn't find any.

We backed off the banks, changed our angles, casted far downstream and ahead of the boat. We lengthened leaders and changed tippet sizes. We changed tactics, going subsurface. We tried sinking lines of various densities, tried different flies through the same runs, opening and closing fly boxes rapidly. Nothing worked. The boat was quiet and melancholy when we pulled into the takeout that evening. Without saying a word, Drew got out and began walking to get the truck and trailer. I stayed seated in the boat, watching the water and wondering what the hell had just happened.

Suddenly, a low rumble came from around the bend. A forty-foot, bright yellow, overloaded party barge with Wisconsin and American flags flapping off its stern appeared and slowly made its way upstream. I watched as the driver picked his course, and eventually, he was directly in front of the boat launch, in mid-river. Noticing me, he waved. I nodded. Then he killed the engine, walked to the bow, and picked up an anchor fit for an ocean liner.

KABOOM!

After the yacht came tight to anchor, the man—apparently an angler—set up a camp chair, removed his shirt, grabbed a spinning rod, sat down, and made a cast toward what looked to be nowhere in particular. Three cranks later, a smallmouth broke the surface. The angler shot me a thumbs up.

"Angling expertise," Sheridan Anderson writes, "is a highly coordinated synthesis of skillful casting, imaginative stalking, keen vision, quick reflexes, plenty of savvy and lots of experience." Of those elements, I suppose "imaginative stalking" leaves the most to personal interpretation.

21
CONTACTS

My eyes open and see black. I blink, an attempt to better my focus or change the result. Still black. Brief disorientation.

Where am I?

I'm in the bed of my truck, and it's early enough that there's no difference in the amount of light inside my eyelids or out. I check the time on my phone. The alarm will go off in six minutes. So, this is it—this is how much sleep I'm getting. I can't fall asleep again, but still, I lie there, unmoving. I think of the things I need to do next, in somewhat short order: make coffee, break camp, hitch the boat, drive to the put-in.

The alarm goes off.

Sitting up, I look through the truck cap's windows. Still black. No signs of headlights from the others. The guys I camped with are fishing elsewhere today. I snicker to myself, calling them lazy, though I'm slightly jealous they're still asleep.

I start boiling water and walk to the restroom at the campground. I haven't camped here since last winter, so just now I notice that the facilities have been improved. The bathroom is bright and, unbelievably, heated. I'm suddenly warmer than I've been since I left home early yesterday morning. I perform the necessaries, brush my teeth, and find my contact case. The contacts are stuck to the sides and look like they've been there for months, not hours.

They're greasy and blurry. Flakes of dirt or, whatever they are, hover in the contact solution. I look at my hands, also greasy and dirty. I think about what was on my fingers when I removed these contacts, the remnants from the previous day's fishing and evening's camping: dirt, river water, fish slime, burger grease, kindling splinters, blood—a long list, and hand soap is not on it. My eyeballs sting and water when the contacts are in. I blink repeatedly, adjust my brow, and the contacts find their fit. Focus.

"I need to replace these tomorrow," I think.

Returning home late that night, I make a small effort to pull some things out of the truck, but bed—a real bed—is calling. The day ends in another bathroom, and again I'm looking at my contact case and the hands that will remove the contacts from my eyeballs. My hands look as bad as they did eighteen hours prior. Soap and water don't make much difference, and my eyes wince as I pull the first lens out. I look at it on my index finger. It's a wonder I don't have more issues with my eyes. A few feet away is the toilet, a fine final resting place for used contacts. I start to flick it in, then pause.

I think of the sights that have passed through this contact during the past few days. Perfect steelhead water. Good friends casting, stepping, and swinging in front of me. Blue skies breaking through morning mist, moss-covered trees, snow-capped mountains, bald eagles, the bow of my boat from the rower's seat. A campfire, surrounded by friends in camp chairs. First light at the put-in, last light at the take-out. If I discard these contacts, do those sights go with them? I gently drop the contact back into the case.

Monday morning, again in the bathroom. The same grubby contacts in the same overused contact case. If I'm going to replace this set, now would be the time. I forgo the opportunity, electing instead to use the pair that helped me see all those great things over the weekend. Perhaps, in some way, looking through these lenses another day or two will keep me in that river, at that place.

Perhaps I'll still see things the way I did when I was out there, instead of the way they actually are as I hunker down into my desk chair.

22
ON TIME

Time surfaces again and again as an intriguing and fluid element in angling. There are the ebbs and flows of passing time, but also recurring themes related to timing, all of which add to the greater sum of fly fishing. No matter how long the actual fishing day, the events that transpire have a decided effect on how long it feels. And rarely are the reality and perception of time in alignment, which suggests that it's unnecessary or inconsequential altogether.

In regard to keeping time, watches are the classic device. I've fished with and without one over the past couple decades, and a finite measurement of time is an interesting addition. On some days, it is a critical piece for rendezvous purposes or minding water flow changes. On others, it seems the watch serves only as a way to verify how time can be distorted while on the water. Guessing the hour after fishing for a while is always good for a laugh, but I don't recommend it when you said you were going to be somewhere at a specific time.

* * *

The day and date were long forgotten, but I knew where I was going and how long I'd be there. Staring at my bulging backpack leaning against the van, I went through a mental checklist of gear, clothing, and food. I was a month into my four-month-long South Island trip and had my backpacking routine mostly dialed. I suppose there wasn't much room for error, really: I didn't have all that much stuff with me to begin with, and most of it was coming along for the hike anyway.

Along with the backpack, I'd been wearing the L.L.Bean fishing vest that my parents gave me when I was a boy, and had been growing into ever since. Before arriving in New Zealand, I hadn't anticipated wearing it much because I thought that I'd be hiking more than changing flies or fiddling with rigging. But that idea revealed itself to be only partly true—I hiked a lot *and* changed flies a lot (and fiddled with rigging a lot, too). When hiking to those backcountry huts, the trail oftentimes followed a river, so I'd wear my backpack over my fishing vest, have a rod rigged, and look for fish on the way there. The fit was a bit awkward, but it worked well enough.

In the vest, among other questionably necessary accessories, was a watch face. I'd tucked it in there specifically before I left the States, and it turned out to be fairly handy, or at least amusing. With it, I'd estimate remaining hiking distances, justify the timing of a meal or snack, or note how long I'd worked a single fish. My desires to possess a time-keeping machine were mixed, but I ended up including it because it seemed like the responsible thing to do. If I did get lost, I'm not sure what good it would've been to know the hour, but I guess if you don't know where you are, it is better to know the time than to know neither.

Satisfied enough with my packing, I started hiking. It was seven miles to the hut. I checked the watch face and estimated that I could be there by noon, but if I spotted some fish along the way, then who knew?

At the first trail marker, I decided to measure my pace. I opened the small vest pocket where the watch face lived, but it wasn't there. I searched all the pockets of my vest but couldn't find it. I stopped hiking and assessed the situation: the trailhead was miles back; the watch held no real financial or sentimental value for me; knowing the time wasn't going to change my behavior, at least in the short term. I took this all to mean I was simply not meant to know the time on the trip, and continued on. When it doesn't matter what time you get to where you're going, what good is a watch anyway?

Later in the New Zealand trip, once Lucas had arrived, we took a break for lunch one day in early afternoon. We'd each caught a few fish already and, for various reasons, Lucas decided that he was done for the day. The bite seemed to be on, though, and I elected to keep fishing upstream. We were in the backcountry and camping for the night, so we came up with a plan to meet back up in an hour or so, which would give me three or four more pools to fish.

My premonition was right: every good-looking pool I came to had a feeding fish in it. Unsurprisingly, I lost track of time. And, without the watch face, I had no way to check it.

When I realized all this, I should've turned around immediately. Still, fishing one more pool seemed prudent, so I continued upstream. Sure enough, I found another rising fish, but didn't catch it. Now external forces were in play. I couldn't force myself to end the day on an unsuccessful note, so I kept going. You can imagine what I saw in the next pool. And the next one.

By the time I did find Lucas, I was beyond late and, justifiably, he was pissed. Not only was my extreme tardiness just plain rude, but it was potentially dangerous as Lucas had been placed in the position of deciding what to do next. Had I gotten lost or injured? Should he stay in place and wait, or go looking for me? I don't remember how much time passed before he cooled off enough to ask how the fishing had been, but by then he probably could've guessed.

* * *

Because fishing guides—in addition to their role in helping you catch fish—also play the parts of therapist and coach, they will sometimes proclaim one time of day to be better than another. When the client needs a boost in confidence or reassurance that they are doing the right things and their lack of success isn't their own fault, a reference to timing can help. A certain hatch will come off, the tide will change, the sun gets above or below a certain level, or a particular stretch of river is reached all at precise times—and when that happens, the fishing will then get better, perhaps much better. Or maybe the guide is reassuring themselves. In any case, when a guide says that it's about time for the fishing to turn on, we take their word for it and focus.

In my own guiding days, our team prided ourselves on bold watch tans burned onto our wrists with help from the cheapest waterproof Walmart model we could find. Our tans served as a sort of badge and measure of expertise. We were staff guides at a guest ranch, and our clients had a fairly strict meal schedule, so we had to keep an eye on the time or risk reprimand from the chef and ranch manager. As such, I can disclose that a guide frequently checking their watch is probably on their game, but, depending on the day and the client, it's also possible that they are counting down to happy hour.

On the Oregon coast, I went winter steelheading with guides Kate and Justin Crump and found their approach to scheduling particularly refreshing. Instead of racing to the boat ramp in an attempt to be the first ones down the river, they intentionally come in last, letting the timing of their fishing sort itself out. As a result, the vast majority of other anglers are already far downstream by the time they get on the water, and they rarely see other boats. For their clients, this means that the stress of angling around others is gone, and the result is an incredibly relaxed and immersive fishing experience.

Justin also pointed out to me that the scramble to be the first to fish certain water is a race that can be won, but it quickly leads to a dead end. While you're fishing that first spot, other boats pass you by on the way to *their* own unfished water, leaving you with…what? If your primary objective is to fish water that hasn't been fished by others, then after you've fished the piece you "won," what next? After several days of fishing on this 'schedule,' I came to appreciate its merits…but that's not to say that I didn't have daily spells of anxiety. "Aren't we supposed to be fishing right now?" I found myself wondering.

* * *

There is a distinct moment of time in fly fishing that requires complete control and patience: when the angler waits to set the hook on a large, dry fly-eating trout. In such instances, time creeps along while the jaws close. Cutthroat are notoriously slow eaters, but big browns may take the prize. It's common knowledge that anglers in New Zealand are advised to say, "God save the Queen" before striking, but I was never able to spit out the words. My approach is to stare stupefied at the eat, and hope that some sort of muscle memory kicks in at just the right time.

Witnessing an early hook-set is painful, especially when the trigger-puller knows what they've done. Words meant for consoling are rarely well-received. Once, after watching a friend blow three consecutive hook-sets on cooperative browns, the only thing I could think to say was, "Hey, you should wait longer." The friend's glare relayed to me that the comment wasn't received as constructive advice, though I swear I was trying to be helpful. Practice may be the only way to get better at this sort of timing, so the more you do it wrong, the more motivation you have to keep trying.

Time may pass in the most curious of ways while swinging flies for anadromous fish, though. It's no secret that steelhead and salmon don't come easily to a fly presentation, so there's ample time between encounters for contemplation while watching your line come around to the hang down, cast after cast. A single swing alone offers up plenty of time for one thought to lead to another, yet in reality, it may only last twenty or thirty seconds. After a day of steelheading, I'll sometimes wonder what I thought about while I stood there in the river, my fly swimming through the currents. Though the exact thoughts are lost, they were mine at the time, so they must still be with me somewhere.

One could say that it takes a certain number of minutes to fish a steelhead run, but I once heard a guide describe this time by the number of cigarettes he could smoke while fishing it. Large steelhead rivers are sometimes described by how many runs you can reasonably fish in a day's light. No matter how you measure it, when you do see one or have an encounter, time is instantly warped. Suddenly, the fishless day you were thinking about giving up on now doesn't seem long enough.

* * *

In spring, a new fishing season has anglers out of bed before sunrise to maximize their fishing day and get in all the daylight they can. Conversely, long summer days can make an angler a little lazy. In some places, you can hit the water at noon and still fish for ten hours. Fall fishing is somewhere in between—you need to wait a little while for the river to warm up a bit, but the window is short before the shadows get long. On winter outings, it's so cold that you swear you've been standing in the water for a couple of hours, only to check the time and see that mere minutes have passed. Either scenario might be beneficial or disastrous: more time on the water could warm things up, literally and figuratively, or you may have already missed the bite completely.

Sitting on a riverside rock, waiting for sunrise and enough light to see the water, time crawls. Then, all of a sudden, you should've been casting fifteen minutes ago. In the evenings, time seems to race when you're looking at a setting sun and failing light. You can see the tailout or the next pool ahead, but you're not sure if you'll make it there before dark. It took forever to get to dusk, but it came and went before you knew it. Or maybe it's the opposite: the afternoon hatch sped by, and now the only thing keeping you from dinner and a cold one is a sun that won't set.

Angling surely has its own way with time. Perhaps all we can say is that it just simply passes. When we're on river time, we can't schedule or reschedule anything, and we get there when we arrive. Time-keeping instruments, inventions, and intentions are sometimes helpful, but they're not necessary.

Galactic hitchhiker Ford Prefect put it this way: "Time is an illusion. Lunchtime, doubly so." The natural world's agenda is far greater and more important than our own.

"Resistance," as Ford's captors say, "is useless!"

23
EVEN BIGGER

It was our fifth day of eight on the river. That wild, mighty, spectacular, and famous river; the one that makes you feel utterly insignificant and that breaks your heart to leave. The one with the falls and the summer run steelhead as big as winters.

British Columbia's incomparable Dean River.

I lucked out and was offered the remaining spot on a do-it-yourself camp trip with three others, two of which I hadn't met in person until we started loading up the cargo baskets on the chopper; one I hadn't even communicated with before arriving at the hangar. But after four, fifteen-hour days of fishing, it was as if we had all grown up together.

By the fifth day, everyone had landed a few fish, so we were relaxed and building some confidence in the water and our approaches. We were also ready to start exploring, so early that morning, two of us—Jack and I—took off on foot upstream on an old logging road that follows the river. With us, we brought one of the small, inflatable rafts that we'd flown in, planning to float and fish our way back to camp over the course of the day.

When the road dead-ended upstream a few miles, the water we found there was the best we'd seen all trip, which was hard to believe given how much good water was downstream. Maybe we were just that excited by *more* amazing water. A giant gravel bar system lay before us with several braids of varying size meandering through. Each braid looked to have two or three runs worth fishing. A quarter-mile downstream, the braids all converged and then split again into two, a large mid-river island separating the two channels. The majority of the flow went around the left side of the island, and even from our distance, we could tell a beautiful run was there. Knowing more water we couldn't see was still downstream, plus the fact that we had two more days to fish, we decided to float down to the island and start there.

Reaching the head of the island, Jack and I stashed the raft and then climbed up a colossal log jam to get a better view of things. From the top, we stared down the length of a massive, classic riffle-run-tailout. The bucket itself looked as long as a football field. I won the roshambo and almost felt guilty about it. Almost.

Making my way down the run, I fished carefully. Each swing felt better than the previous, and I became certain that I was going to get one on every cast. The further downstream I stepped, the more my focus narrowed and my pulse quickened. Eventually, I was getting close to the end of it and started judging how many more casts I had left. If it doesn't happen now, then when? I looked upstream, hoping to see Jack hooked up, thinking maybe I'd just missed the fish.

As I came into the tailout, one swing slowly came across and into tension. It was an odd feeling, kind of like my fly had swung directly into a big, submerged tree. I raised my rod slowly, and the tension remained, but gave slightly. I started reeling in, thinking that this big branch I'd snagged was now coming up from the bottom of the river.

"Is that a fish?!" Jack yelled from upstream.

I shook my head, but I wasn't sure. I kept reeling, the tension held, and my rod flexed deeper. Then, a distinct head shake, and another. I shouted something incoherent and heard Jack start crashing downstream toward me.

The way it fought, I thought it was a Chinook. It never made a long, fast run but constantly bulldogged me, barely giving an inch at a time. Slowly, with encouragement from Jack and as much side-pressure as I dared, we brought the fish into the shallows. There, it rolled, and we got our first look at the giant, wild buck.

After six nerve-racking rounds of fighting the fish to hand, barely getting a finger on it, followed by the fish confidently and steadily running back to the bottom of the middle of the river, we had him. My hand barely fit around the base of its tail. Only five miles from the ocean, the buck was tinted, as if by watercolors. Down its body, green faded to pink and then silver; the pink stripe led to bold, cherry cheeks. It was most likely the largest steelhead I will ever hold in my hands. In awe, we stared, unblinking, and then watched as he disappeared back into the aquamarine of that wild, mighty, spectacular, and famous river.

Then, to my surprise, instead of jumping right back in the run in hopes of hooking his own, Jack sat down on a log next to me to talk about how it all had happened.

"What do you do after you land a fish like that?" we asked each other.

We go fishing in distant destinations for the fish. We want the challenge of finding them, hooking them, and bringing them to hand. We want to witness them ourselves, behold their beauty, and see how big they can get. But in the process of pursuing our intentions—an encounter with the fish we imagine—we find that the fish become secondary to the *unexpected* encounters we find along the way, like new friends, surprising conversations, little epiphanies, and big shared moments.

I've since landed large and meaningful fish in other faraway places that felt similarly, and I now think that the answer to our question, "What do you do after you land a fish like that?" is this: you watch your friend fish and hope like hell that they get one even bigger.

24
THE DAY BEGINS THE NIGHT BEFORE

The day begins the night before. Timeless questions consume us before morning's departure and fall into three categories. The natural: *'Where to go?'* The psychological: *'When to begin?'* And the supernatural: *'How to prepare?'*

Some anglers include all categories in their analysis, with simplifications and elaborations. Others rely solely on the oft-referenced and ever-opaque "gut feeling." Eventually, decisions are made—sometimes casually, sometimes in excruciating fashion. Today, it is the latter. For me, gut feelings are restricted to hunger, hangovers, or nerves.

Drift boat in tow, my driver approaches a turn that signifies the decision between floating one of two rivers. Conversation stops. Everyone squirms in their seats, and we look at each other, head-scratching compulsively. When it seems too late to make the turn, the driver jumps on the brakes. Then, muttering unintelligibly, hits the gas again.

At the put-in, another quandary arises: the start of our float downstream determines when we'll reach certain points on the float, so when should we launch? Bugs might be hatching right now, but we want high sun for the long, grassy bank full of hoppers and afternoon shade for the riffles where the caddis pop. Reaching the take-out before pitch-dark is always nice. Should we kill time or rush to the water? No one knows or can decide, so the boat is made ready in a throw-it-all-in, hurry-up-and-wait, tire-kicking pace.

We make our final preparations, and each of us tends to rituals and superstitions. Which beat-up, faded fishing hat will I wear today? Pack my raincoat so it doesn't rain. Should I bring the extra rod, my favorite and oldest one—the one reserved for small dry flies that I haven't used yet this summer? I can't envision the scenario of needing it today, but I grab it anyway. Was that a gut feeling? Or just the fear of being under-prepared?

Finally, the boat drifts away from the put-in and indecision. No more planning or pondering. Now it's recognition and reaction. The fish are here, and they will eat, provided we give them what they want, how they want it. The perfect dry fly, if dragging, is as appetizing as a bacon jalapeno cheeseburger served atop a stinking, soiled garbage can lid.

Sometimes, the angles appear plain as day: a mayfly hatches, floats downstream, and is eaten; a fish in the seam, spotted from the high bank, white mouth opening and closing; bank-side brush crawling with stoneflies. Other times, the formula is more cryptic: a picture-perfect pool, but no bugs, fish, nor even a breeze; a hatch as thick as smoke, yet not a fish to be seen.

Floating downstream, I make note of what I can, take my best guess, and test a theory. My presentation is made—a specific fly, in a specific way—and the feedback is immediate. I catch one on my fifth cast, a gorgeous, native Yellowstone cutthroat, a golden agate against the cool, blue-green water. They get bigger than this one, but I'm not sure if they get prettier.

Spirits soar as the sun reaches its peak. Rounding a bend in the river, a shaded bank awaits—the ideal viewpoint to watch the water and prepare our riverside feast. Cold drinks for everyone, passed around like a bucket brigade; a potluck of homemade selections curated through years of riverside feeds, each item perfectly balancing taste, shareability, and cooler space. Soon, full bellies and the early-morning departure catch up to everyone. My eyelids become heavy. I pull down the brim of whichever hat I chose that morning.

Cottonwood leaves rustle in the afternoon breeze, allowing beams of sunlight to alight onto my face, deep in siesta. I stir, vaguely aware of the surroundings but still half-asleep. Suddenly, a distinctive sound snaps me awake: fly line ripped off the water, setting the hook.

Nap time is over. Everybody back in the boat.

As afternoon turns toward evening, the catching follows the sun's declining course. Thunderheads stage in the mountains, ready to color a sunset to match the hues along the gill plates of the day's trout. I feel the conditions change—temperature, pressure, wind direction—and it suddenly becomes unclear which will make it to the take-out first: the brewing storm or our boat.

Acknowledging the failing light, more than a day's share of fish, and the approaching weather, the angler in the bow sits down and slowly reels in—the most definitive indication that their fishing day is done. The rower stops pulling on the oars, and our vessel quietly assumes the speed of the current. I make a few nonchalant, target-less casts from the stern, more on principle than desire.

With the take-out in sight, it appears we've avoided a drenching after all. But, while the rower pushes toward the ramp, all our eyes zero-in on a rise downstream. The rower softly slows the boat. Everyone's thinking the same thing: *Come up again.*

The trout obliges with a confident rise, nose breaking the surface, followed by the dorsal, and finally a large tail. The whole process takes four full seconds. It's a good one.

"One more time," someone says. "I dare you."

A lingering minute passes. Thunder growls in the distance, and a flash lights the mountainside.

"Do it."

Gulp.

"Thank you."

The rower eases the boat into position and lowers the anchor inaudibly.

"You're up," they say, and I realize they're talking to me.

From a previously unseen box, they produce a fly.

"You want to tie it on?"

The trout rises again, and I show them my shaking hands.

I watch as they rig my favorite dry fly rod—the one I almost didn't bring—from leader to tippet to fly. Knots cinched, I take the rod in one hand, the fly in the other, and inspect it. It is clearly a custom tie, saved for this exact time and place. The moment has materialized, a function of all the variables analyzed and over-analyzed. Here, now, and with good fortune. Another rise.

I start casting. When I have the distance, I make one more false cast to ensure placement and let it drop. All eyes watch it fall. All eyes see it land six feet upstream of the fish, right in its lane.

I throw a mend and feed line. The fly is drifting right over its head.

It's the end of a day that began the night before, and everyone freezes.

25

ANADROMOUS ADORATION

"He's going to lose it," Paul said.

I spun around to face him, and stared. Those were blasphemous words. How could he—or anyone, for that matter—possibly utter such a thing while our comrade was tight to a fish that usually exists only in dreams? To say something like that was more than sabotage—it was nothing short of *sacrilege*.

"His mind, I mean!" Paul blurted. "He's going to lose his mind. Not, you know..." He referred here to the fish, of course, but wouldn't let himself say it out loud.

Alex, meanwhile, was holding his ground. The long Spey rod was bent all the way to the handle, which he held tightly with both hands. Thirty feet away in the aquamarine river, a large winter steelhead rolled and broke the surface, giving all of us our first look. The fish was so bright that it looked like an oval vanity mirror tumbling amidst the emerald currents.

A minute later, and it was all over—in the net. Alex fell to his knees in front of it, staring at the incredible fish. We watched as he drank deep from the cocktail of emotions that had been brewing since his last steelhead three years prior. Three years of casts, schemes, hopes, dreams, early-morning and late-night conversations, studies, almosts, and so many heartbreaks. It all culminated and now concluded.

When you love something, it's impossible to predict how you will react in the moment that you are directly exposed to that thing and your cup runs over. Some are speechless, some scream, some laugh hysterically, some blather incoherently. Alex's moment came and quietly, he wept.

Wild winter steelhead, like the one Alex encountered that day in March on the Oregon coast, are among a certain class of fish unto themselves. They behave in the most curious, unique, and moving ways. In fact, the fish themselves are always moving, but it's the magnitude and nature of their journey that inspires others to care about and care for them. Anadromous fish are species that hatch and, some years later, spawn and then expire in the exact same small, freshwater stream.

In between, they live a precarious and itinerant life, migrating to and from the ocean where they feed and mature enough to reproduce. Along their journey, they face obstacles both natural and man-made: predators, dams, warming water, waterfalls, food shortages, environmental disasters, and degraded habitats, among others. Some anadromous fish travel thousands of miles across open ocean during their lifespan and yet are still able to locate and return to their natal waters to spawn. Others attempt equally lengthy journeys, only to be met by concrete barriers and various forms of artificial, suboptimal fish passages.

These fish also serve as critical fuel for the ecosystems that rear them. Between the times when anadromous fish leave their home streams and when they return, they consume prey in the ocean, absorbing nutrients that are later given back to the river and its neighboring flora. Which is to say nothing of the dozens of other animals and insects which feast directly on their carcasses after the journey. Compare that type of afterlife to being put in a wooden box and buried, for example.

But anadromous fish aren't programmed to only sleep in one bed. Every year, a small percentage of each distinct subspecies become "strays," meaning they do not go back to their natal streams to spawn. In an effort to ensure their species' survival, they hedge their bets and intentionally travel somewhere else. This is especially important today as climate change and warming waters reduce the southern limits of some species. Those same forces that melt ice caps may make more northern rivers habitable for the first time, leading stray anadromous fish to start colonizing new rivers.

As further testament to their resilience, consider the anadromous fish of the Olympic Peninsula's Elwha River. When I first moved to Washington in 2011, efforts were well underway to remove the Glines Canyon and Elwha dams from the river. By 2014, both were gone, and within six months, the National Park Service, NOAA, and others observed winter and summer steelhead, as well as Chinook, pink, and coho salmon passing the former downstream dam site. None of those fish had been in that stretch of river since 1910. Chinook salmon were observed above the upstream dam site only ten days after removal; summer steelhead, once thought to be extinct in that river, have since returned. More recently, on California and Oregon's Klamath River, only months after removal of four dams—Iron Gate, Copco No. 1 and 2, and J.C. Boyle dams—Chinook salmon were recorded in spawning tributaries above the former uppermost dam site. It's clear: demolish the dam, and the fish will come back.

I first became aware of anadromous fish in college. As an undergrad, I studied Atlantic salmon and their struggles, reading about the effects of dams on anadromous fish populations. I surveyed anglers on their experiences and examined dam removals and the results on related fisheries and communities. As compelling and influential as it all was, it was still academic, conceptual; words on a page. Like listening to sports commentators debate the merits of a player, a team, or a game that just ended, there is a level of understanding only available to those who have played the sport themselves. Similarly, it took a decade of living in the Pacific Northwest for me to truly appreciate anadromous fish.

Ultimately, I came to adore everything about them and all the obscure elements that go into fly fishing for them. If I were to describe the experience in a single word, I'd call it *inspiring*. Hooking a steelhead in a Columbia River tributary and realizing that fish has traveled over five hundred miles, passing dams, nets, anglers, and predators, to meet you at that point—that's inspiring. Spending a week in a steelhead camp with a group of anglers who get up in the dark and fish until last light, regardless of whether they're finding fish or not—that's inspiring. Learning that some rivers have counts of Atlantic salmon that are measured in double digits, and yet numerous individuals still make it their life's work to protect those fish? That's inspiring.

If I were to describe anadromous fish in two words, I'd say *beyond belief*. Have you ever hooked a salmon that seemed like it was swimming downstream at full speed, even though you're positive that it's migrating upstream? That's beyond belief. Standing knee deep in a steelhead river and realizing that the mountains on either side of you are a thousand times taller than you are? Holding an impossibly bright, wild winter steelhead in a river and realizing that it was swimming in the ocean that same day? That's beyond belief.

Amazements of salmon and steelhead and their environs aside, across the West Coast, fishing closures are now commonplace due to low populations of wild anadromous fish. Every year, anglers have to wonder and watch if the rivers they adore are even going to be open to fishing or not. As a single example, look at the counts of wild steelhead passing over the Bonneville Dam on the Columbia River; in the last five years, these numbers are roughly half of the previous twenty-five-year average—not to mention comparisons to historic abundance or predevelopment (before 1850) population estimates, which are far bleaker. Despite this widespread regional decline, as of 2025, it remains legal for sport anglers to harvest wild steelhead in southern Oregon for part of the year. That's beyond belief.

And if I were to describe the effect these amazing fish have had on my life in three words… *on my mind.* Atlantic salmon were on my father's mind before I was born, and on his father's and his uncle's before he was born. In returning home to the Northeast after more than a decade in the Pacific Northwest, I was granted the opportunity to again angle for the fish of my youth: brilliantly gorgeous native brook trout, happy and hungry smallmouth bass, wild and leaping landlocked salmon, and brute but discriminating stripers. What a pleasure it was to get reacquainted. But anadromous Atlantic salmon, a species that I'd still never fished for, were heavy on my mind, consuming most of my angling mindshare.

So, when I received an invitation from a new friend to fish for them in New Brunswick, I had to accept. This despite the fact that, at the time, even getting into Canada wasn't possible. Months later, after barely avoiding a debacle at the border thanks to time-sensitive COVID tests, I arrived and got my first look at the famous Miramichi River. What I found was a vast, wild river filled with migratory fish, a rich and robust angling past and present, and a passionate cast of characters there to share and adore it all with. What more could an angler ask for?

Also on my mind leading up to and during that trip was my late great-uncle Charlie, a lifelong Mainer, keen Northeast outdoorsman, and dedicated Atlantic salmon angler. A weathered copy of Joe Brooks' *Trout Fishing* served as his fishing journal; my father keeps it in his bookcase still to this day. On the inside cover and over its pages, Charlie documented decades of Atlantic salmon fishing trips with his friends across Maine and on the Miramichi. It only takes a quick scan of his numbers to see that he was usually top rod.

These facts—that Uncle Charlie fly fished for Atlantic salmon often, caught a lot, and usually the most—sit nicely with me. I only hope that I've somehow inherited some of his angling abilities—genetically, spiritually, or however the case may be. I'm inclined to say that Uncle Charlie was a 'good' or 'great' salmon angler based simply on these facts alone, but at the same time, I'm left wondering what makes a good anadromous angler in general. Furthermore, what makes a good anadromous angler these days?

When it comes to landing an anadromous fish like a steelhead, Atlantic salmon, Chinook salmon, or sea-run brown trout, it's the most devoted who get rewarded. There is no better tactic than time spent in pursuit. But even if devotion is the singular, most effective strategy, that only gets us so far. Assuming that we can't (or don't) fish every day of the season, we have to be very smart about it, too—using all the available tools in a logical manner. There are countless data sets and collections of information accessible to anyone with the motivation to find them. Historical and real-time fish counts, overlaid with weather forecasts, water flows, and flow forecasts, offer powerful arguments on where to be fishing and when. Or, if you're more inclined to read how-to books, take your pick; in my experience, one often leads to another. If you're able to fish with an experienced guide and willing to accept constructive criticism, you'll undoubtedly find that fruitful as well.

Is that it, then? Be devoted and well-informed? Certain tackle evolutions are undeniably more effective than others, so why not also arm ourselves with as many of the most sophisticated tools that we can? We'll certainly make some friends at the local fly shop in the process (and it probably doesn't *hurt*), but bear in mind that it's foolhardy to have faith that the next best thing will directly correlate to more fish being caught. I'd rather not fish with bamboo or fiberglass if I have a choice, but I would, and I'm certain that there are plenty of anglers who have caught many more salmon and steelhead than I ever will using rods made from those materials.

Still, when you're standing in the river, the tackle does not cast or fish itself. I once asked a lifetime steelhead angler and guide if he thought that there was a specific fly pattern or style or other piece of tackle—existing or not—that offered an advantage over other anglers. I swear, I wasn't asking for a silver bullet, but I realize now that's probably how it came out.

His answer, honest, thorough, and detailed, essentially translated to: "Just fish better." Another steelhead guide, who spent the balance of his year as a hotshot firefighter, put it this way: "It's not the tool that moves the dirt, it's the human."

What about the less-scientific, more mystical elements? My good fishing friend Patrick told me that in preparation for a winter steelhead season, he once took a dozen recently-tied flies and drove them as far upstream in one particular drainage as he could. Then, he soaked the flies in a known spawning tributary. The idea was to impart the tributary's "scent" into the flies so that, when swung near a steelhead downstream in that same drainage, they'd be inspired to take the fly. This theory includes several assumptions that are probably impossible to confirm (or deny), but nothing that any optimistic angler can't get behind fairly easily. The experiment was inconclusive—which is to say, he didn't hook any on those flies—but it still might be the best idea ever.

There's also the tried-and-true tactic of pulling inspiration and fortune from the fly you choose. I've fished with flies tied by close friends, late friends, and famous-in-my-eyes folks, and it feels good and right, like I'm fishing with them. Such flies are irreplaceable, though, so the fishing is riskier. Losing one results in a degree of heartbreak depending on the connection to the tyer and also how much confidence you had in the specific pattern at that moment.

Choice of fly can be critical or irrelevant, depending on the day and, more so, the fish. To keep things simple, I suggest picking what has worked before, what you like the looks of, or what a more experienced angler suggests—conveniently, there's usually overlap. On the banks of the Miramichi, an older local salmon angler told me that over the course of a fishing season several decades ago, he'd caught a hundred salmon in the pool I'd just been fishing, and he did it all on two patterns. "Any fly so long as it's an Undertaker or a Green Machine," he said. I'd just landed a fish on a Silver Rat, and when my guide informed him of this fact, the local looked at me like I was the luckiest fisherman that he'd ever seen. Whichever pattern you choose, just keep it in the water as much as possible.

For several years in a row, I fished for winter steelhead with my good friend James, and his father, Ed. Ed's a less experienced angler but loves being on the water. For the first few years, whenever we got to the river, I'd proudly offer him the choice of a half-dozen intricate, freshly-tied patterns that I had confidence in. Unfortunately, none of them ever worked. So, at the start of our trip the following year, when I again offered him a choice of fly to use, Ed pushed back.

"You never give me any flies that work!" he said, chuckling.

Ed was mostly kidding, but I realized that giving him the option to choose what looked or felt best—what, to my mind, would give him *more* confidence—was having the opposite effect. So, I pulled out an unsophisticated, beat-up leech pattern that I'd caught a fish on several weeks prior.

"This one has been in a steelhead's mouth," I offered. "Is that good enough?"

He took it without hesitation.

When describing the potential productivity of an anadromous fishery or relaying appropriate expectations for a day fishing for anadromous species, "encounter" is often the preferred term (as opposed to "catches.") As in, "one encounter per day." What I love about this phrase is that it all but suggests you won't land one, but, with luck, you'll come to know that one was there. An encounter could be a grab that immediately sticks, a hard-fought battle taking you downstream over boulders and around logs, and an incredible fish in the net. The encounter could also be a pluck of your fly, just enough to pull four inches of line off your reel, and then…nothing. Or an encounter may come after you've fished through a gorgeous tailout when, on your hike back up the bank, you see one roll where you were just casting. Or maybe you just stepped into the run, and roll casted your leader and a couple feet of line downstream, straightening it out before making your first cast; you begin to pick it up to cast, and one is on. In all instances, there it was.

Eventually, you reach the point where you've done all you can or all you can think to do. Any anadromous angler knows that sometimes the fish just aren't there. But do we ever know, in certainty, that they're there or not, right this minute? When all it takes is one fish to make the day, what good is that information anyway? How many does it take to offer hope or, better yet, confidence? Ten thousand fish in the river? One thousand? A hundred? Ten?

And what if there actually were just ten? Or even just one? Would we still go? What if there were none? At some point, if we are to consider ourselves "good" anadromous anglers—honest and aware—instead of asking ourselves, "What are my chances?" we must ask, "What are the fish's chances?" Just asking the question may feel foreign enough, but considering the potential results if the question goes unanswered proves more than motivating.

If we are considering the fish's chances, why not use the same approach that we use for ourselves? Just as in our own angling, there is no silver bullet. But if we apply our devotion, knowledge of when to go and when not to, bringing with us all the most sophisticated tools we can, plus a little mystic and magic, then we'll give the fish the best chance. For wild anadromous fish, giving them the best chance translates into habitat restorations, policy changes and updates, dam removals, safe catch and release techniques, and science-based hatchery practices. Ironically, I believe that if we've done all that and continue to do all that, we'll truly be "fishing" better.

Even with all these efforts, it's not enough for a steelhead or salmon river to exist today without more help. It takes the dedicated and often thankless work of agencies, departments, organizations, Tribes, and individuals to ensure that healthy populations and fisheries remain intact. So, what to do? An easy place to start is by gaining understanding and awareness. In doing so, we may find that it leads to an affection, perhaps eventually an adoration of anadromous fish. What may follow from there is nothing short of inspiring, in the truest sense of the word.

J. Drew Lanham, an ornithologist, naturalist, and writer, poses a unique approach to conservation: the *head to heart connection*. His theory is that a combination of scientific information and emotional ties to the natural world leads to conservation action; in other words, that which you know about and care about, you *do* something about. Combine this with Robin Wall Kimmerer's approach in her essay "Epiphany in the Beans." Kimmerer, a scientist, professor, and enrolled member of the Citizen Potawatomi Nation, asks the question, "Do you think that the earth loves you back?"

It's easy to wrap your head around the concept of loving anadromous fish—simply look at the lengths we go to try to have an encounter with one. Why? Because of how they make us feel. Landing and releasing one, hooking and losing one, wading and casting in a beautiful river, forming a lifelong friendship while fishing for them, watching your best friends soak in the moment after an encounter… these are all feelings that arise because of anadromous fish. So, considering all that these fish give to *us*, it's not a stretch to think that they might love us, too.

"Knowing that you love the earth changes you, activates you to defend and protect and celebrate," Kimmerer writes. "But when you feel that the earth loves you in return, that feeling transforms the relationship from a one-way street into a sacred bond." A bond, by definition, is something that unites or binds, holding all related parties accountable. I think that a good anadromous angler today works to fulfill their end of the bargain, taking into account what's best for the fish.

Ultimately, that's also what's best for them and their community.

The steelhead Alex caught that day wasn't our only encounter. Twenty minutes earlier, I'd landed a nearly-identical fish in the same run. It was the first steelhead that I'd landed in some time as well, and my first after migrating back to the Pacific Northwest a few months prior. I was still having some mixed emotions about the move, but was slowly getting settled. A day on the water with old friends and a first-hand encounter with a wild, winter steelhead was just the housewarming gift I needed.

A few days after we returned home from that trip, I got a phone call from Alex.

"Hey buddy," he said. "Remember when we both caught steelhead?"

"Sure do," I laughed.

"I loved that."

CONCLUSION: THE BEST FLY FISHING IS EVERYWHERE

It's here.

The best fly fishing is *here*, down the road from home. When you get to the brook, follow it downstream until it meets the main stem. Cross there and fish your way upriver, all the way to the old bridge. There are some good pools below it, but keep going; the best fly fishing is upstream. Wait until dusk, and the red quills will start hatching. Sometimes they don't begin until it's too dark to be able to tie another fly on, so make sure you don't lose the one you have. When they start going, though, it's the best fly fishing. You probably won't catch many, but you won't believe how pretty those old brook trout are.

It's also *here*: where the creek runs into the bay, on the biggest outgoing tides. When the tide is really ripping, it's like a river flowing through the middle of the ocean; like a zipper down the middle of a sweatshirt. Those sea-run cutthroat stack up here—unless it's salmon season and then the coho do. One night, we broke three rods between four of us. The current was too fast and the silvers were too strong and we were too impatient because we wanted to hook another one. It's tough to beat a pink-and-white Clouser minnow here but pink-and-chartreuse usually works just as well too. On the right tide, at the right time of the year, it's the best fly fishing.

You can ride your bike to the best fly fishing too: it's here, in town, just off the bike path. Go slow riding by the duck ponds, wear polarized glasses, and you'll see the big carp. I can't tell you how they got in there but I can tell you what to cast at them. Wait until they tip down, and start tailing—then cast. When you hook one, hold on and hope that they don't take you too far into the weeds. You might even land one!

But the *best* fly fishing is *here*, around the campfire, when everyone's back from the water. That's when the stories get good, and everyone shares some. Numbers and statistics are distorted, and what's true and what's slightly-untrue is hard to discern, but who's to say what really happened? Does it matter anyway? Which is a better fly fishing story, the one that's accurate or the one that's unforgettable? The best fly fishing is always in camp beneath a canopy of old growth that lets a couple bright stars shine through. And, the best fly fishing is also in that same camp the next morning, when only a few are awake. Next to the smudge of a fire, while water boils and the French press waits, you can find out where the best fly fishing was yesterday and where it'll be today...

Like *there.*

Way back in the backcountry, a few miles upriver from the Gulf; the best fly fishing is there. It feels like the mangroves are closing in on you there, and it's tough—for me, at least—to figure out exactly where I am, but the tarpon love it there. When they're in the river, it's kind of like trout fishing for eighty-pounders; it's the best fly fishing. And you know when they're there because they roll as far as you can see. Don't get distracted by watching them roll though, because sooner or later, one will roll within casting distance and you gotta lay your fly down as fast as you can. Making a good cast is hard, but calming your nerves is even harder. The constant commentary from your friends in the boat doesn't make either any easier, but that's why it's the best fly fishing. The only thing about *there*, is you have to fly there. Take the red-eye—it's worth it—then find a good Cuban coffee for the drive across Alligator Alley.

After that, you'll be ready for the best fly fishing. It's *there*, halfway across the globe and in the other hemisphere, so you'll want at least a couple weeks' time to make it worth your while, and to learn the game. You'll spend more time hiking along rivers and looking at rivers than casting into rivers, but when you *are* casting, you'll be able to see exactly what you're trying to catch. And what you're trying to catch is the biggest brown trout you've ever seen, and it's in a foot of water, and it's taking mayfly duns every ninety seconds or so, and it's the best fly fishing. By that point, you're used to casting seventeen-foot leaders into the wind, but you're still learning the timing of the hookset because you've only fed a couple of these giant browns so far. No matter—go ahead and make your first cast, and make sure it's a good one.

Still, the best fly fishing is *there*, in the first miles of the mighty river, with tidewater in sight. The brightest, hottest steelhead are there and they swim right past you, on their way to the falls and the upper river. They take the fly way out in the middle, and then they head for the ocean. If they don't spool you, they take you to your backing twice. After that, they pirouette in midair, and that's when they shake the hook. Charles says it's the best fly fishing, and he knows. There was some staff from the Department of Fisheries and Oceans counting fish when he got there, but they left midweek, which was telling. He caught his first and only in the morning of the day he left, but it was still the best fly fishing.

And *there*, at the long, live-edge dining table, surrounded by a baker's dozen of others you just met but now know well, waiting for the wine to come around; at the horseshoe bar in the middle of the family restaurant with your old fishing friend who's now a local there, after having tonight's special; in the truck cab on the way to the marina, when the sun breaks the horizon and everyone gets their first look, and the coffee-fueled conversation stalls for the first, and only, time; there, in your sleeping bag, on your pad, in a tent on the high bank overlooking the river, your feet and legs exhausted from hiking all morning and then wading all afternoon and evening, but your head and heart alive, awake, and full from flashbacks of the that same long day and visions of the one to follow—that's where the best fly fishing takes place.

The *best* fly fishing? It's everywhere.

The best fly fishing is *everywhere.*

It's a ferry-train-plane-and-automobile-ride away, and it's also on the way home from work.

It happens with your mother, father, grandparent, brother, sister, friend, friends, best friend; with your partner. With a favorite fishing guide, with a good dog, a young child, and the worst fishing guide; a neighbor and a stranger. With memories and ghosts—of others and ourselves.

The fish are everywhere too: the biggest fish, the most fish, the hardest fish, the prettiest fish, the one-and-only, and the one-that-got-away. They can all be found, but only if looked for. We look by going fly fishing.

To find the best *fly fishing*, look anywhere. Look *everywhere.*

I have found it, I keep finding it, and I remain in search for it.

See you there.

ACKNOWLEDGMENTS

This book is the result of the inspiration, fodder, support, encouragement, and combinations thereof provided by hundreds of generous people in my life. My initial attempt to recognize all of those who have, in one way or another, lead to the resulting combination and culmination that you now hold, ultimately failed; there are simply too many to thank. So, suffice to say, if you and I have gone or talked about fishing, exchanged stories verbally and/or in writing, batted ideas back and forth, shared high or low moments, or have at all generally crossed paths, then you are a part of this book, and I am indebted. Thank you. Still, I'd like to specifically acknowledge a number of folks and groups of people.

I am grateful to my parents, Jo Ann and Jon, for many, many things, but especially for sharing a love of nature, waters, and fly fishing. They brought me to rivers, ponds, and woods, fostered my relationships with them, gave me the freedom to explore, and asked me to tell them about it all. My grandparents Elinor and Julius Woolf set inspiring examples as intrepid travelers, as well as curious and creative minds. Marnie was always in favor of a fishing or camping trip, and always welcomed the stories upon return. My paternal grandfather Philip and his brother, Charlie, both keen northeast outdoorsmen and anglers, have influenced me in ways I know and do not know. Thanks to my aunts, uncles, and cousins in Maine, New Jersey, and New York for never-ending love. Thank you to all the chosen family members in Maine that I've known and adventured with on water and over land since I was a child. And much love to the Detwilers, for their consistent encouragement.

When it comes to angling, I have the immeasurable fortune of a lifetime's worth of fishing partners, mentors, guides, and instructors. The majority of the stories contained in this book are a result of outings with these individuals, and my progress as an angler is in direct correlation with their generosity. From a young age and to this day, John Mitton and Jim McGinn have been influential fixtures in my life and fishing life. Early trips with the extended Butler-Martinelli family fueled many campfire tales. Other first fishing friends I hold dear are those I met at Maine Sport: Lucas Young and the late Paul McGurren.

Entering Bates College, my fishing world expanded considerably when I joined a cast of characters that incorporated the infamous Bates Fishing Club; they remain my closest friends. Among Club members, I've spent the most time on the water with a particular group of three, to whom I owe much—we assemble on the water under the name *JACK*—but I extend thanks to all the women and men of the BFC, as well as all my classmates and comrades at Bates for ongoing fellowship. Thanks also to Peter Goldsborough and Sawyer Fahy for help with chapters in this book. Additional thanks to my academic advisor, environmental economist, and friend Lynne Lewis, for her mentorship in what would be my first published article, and for showing me what was possible when combining personal and professional passions.

Moving west, my angling understanding was tested and continued to grow while working at the 4UR Ranch in southwest Colorado. Thanks to my fellow guides for upping my game and for the post-game analyses. Heartfelt thanks to Captain Andy Lee and the Lee family for all their love and the brain sauce.

Despite all I learned while on the way there, my steepest and longest fly fishing learning curve was in the Pacific Northwest while working at Far Bank Enterprises—the umbrella company for the brands Sage, Redington, RIO Products, and Fly Water Travel. Fortunately/unfortunately, there are too many to name from my years there, but thanks to all. A special thanks to those in R&D, as well as Marc Bale, Zack Dalton, and Brian Gies for steady friendship and mentorship on all things related, in some way, to fly fishing (which certainly covers much more than actual fly fishing). Thanks also go to all the independent sales reps and distributors who welcomed me with open arms.

Across the fly fishing industry, I owe many thanks to those who shared insight, kindness, and time on the water, especially Chris Keeley, Matson Rogers, and Kat and Nat Linville. To all the guides I'm so fortunate to have spent time with, thank you for sharing your worlds and your vast knowledge; notably Mark Engler, Scott O'Donnell, Whitney Gould, Mike McCune, Andy Szofran, Chappie Chapman, Stu Tripney, Ray Fecher, Doug Kilpatrick, Kate and Justin Crump, Mark Raisler, and the gentlemen at Country Haven.

Throughout this book's journey, I was encouraged and inspired by, and collaborated with, a plethora of writers, artists, creatives, and creators. Many thanks to these incredibly-talented, hard-working, humble, and supportive individuals. Specifically, I'd like to thank Paul Richardson, Joe Klementovich, Chris Henderson, Wilds Drake, Kyle Schaefer, Breen Nolan, Aya Morton, Marco Materazzi, Ashley Ryall, Carter Thomas, Billy Woodward, Magdalena Wallhoff-Lamprecht, Nick Kelley, and Ryan Heffernan. Likewise, I owe huge thanks to Bre Drake and Chase White for their talents and generosity in the designs and artwork of this book, and for their genuine enthusiasm in the project.

Thanks to my many, many fine fishing friends across the country and the globe—in Maine, New England, Florida, Colorado, Idaho, Montana, Washington, Oregon, and beyond. A big cheers while on one knee to the Ice Boys.

Thanks to Tom Bie at *The Drake* for taking a chance on me, and for years of collaboration and constructive feedback. Gratitude to Jason Rolfe at *The Flyfish Journal* for faith, functional edits, and friendship. Big thanks to Steve Duda for advice, for listening, for reading, for sharing, and for encouragement. Many thanks to John Larison for being willing to share time and wisdom. Thanks to Riverhorse Nakadate, Anne Landfield, Dylan Tomine, Greg Fitz, and the entire *Writers on the Fly* crew; to Chandra Brown and the Freeflow Institute community. And thank you to all the extremely talented editors that provided opportunities and collaborations: Chris Dombrowski, Kirk Deeter, Jimmy Fee, Matt Haeffner, Patrick Washburn, Martin Silverstone, Zack Williams, and Daniel Ritz.

This book would certainly not exist without the dedicated, numerous, and thoughtful reviews from my collection of trusted readers: Alex Blouin, Andy Archer, Bri Dostie, Cameron Scott, Charles Gehr, Chet Clem, Jake Crawford, Kara Armano, Kenny Morrish, and Marc Bale. Thank you all.

Of course, I am also eternally grateful to the team at Hatherleigh Press for their partnership and the opportunity to bring these stories to the page. Thanks to Andrew Flach, Ryan Tumambing, and Ryan Kennedy for all their support and camaraderie.

Still, I owe the most thanks to my partner, Stacey Detwiler. Not only did she contribute to this book in most of the ways described above, but she was also the sole person who rode alongside me for the entirety of its emotional roller coaster. She was, in fact, the engine for parts this journey, and never yielded in her support and belief of it, and of me. Thank you. I love you.

ABOUT THE AUTHOR

Jesse Lance Robbins hails from rural, midcoast Maine, where a love for waters, fly fishing, boating, camping, and nature was passed on by his parents, grandparents, and family friends. Following these passions, he has worked in and lived various facets of fly fishing since high school—from fly shop staff, trout bum, guide, casting instructor, trip host, and writer to tackle design and development, marketing, travel, and sales; for over a decade, he worked in-house at Sage, Redington, RIO Products, and Fly Water Travel. Jesse has over thirty years of fly fishing experience across the United States and five continents, and has found generous mentorship along the way from numerous exceptional and eccentric anglers, casters, and guides.

As an essayist, creative writer, and journalist, Jesse's work has appeared in *The Drake, The Flyfish Journal, Swing the Fly, Atlantic Salmon Journal, Modern Huntsman,* and *TROUT,* among others, and he is a frequent reader and organizer of the Writers on the Fly event series. A 2006 graduate of Bates College, he was president of the infamous Bates Fishing Club, and his thesis on Atlantic salmon and dam removal economics was later published in the *Journal of the American Water Resources Association.* He now works in nonprofit fisheries, river, and water conservation, connecting people with the places they love, and the work being done to protect and restore them. Jesse and his partner Stacey live near the confluence of the McKenzie and Willamette Rivers in Oregon with their cache of old boats, timeless books, acoustic guitars, and always-strung fly rods.

For more on Jesse, see:
www.jesselancerobbins.com and @jesse.lance.robbins.